GRIT,

GRACE

AND

HUSTLE

A FAITH GAL'S GUIDE TO AUTHENTIC SUCCESS

BY: RACHEL REVA

Ark House Press
PO Box 1722, Port Orchard, WA 98366 USA
PO Box 1321, Mona Vale NSW 1660 Australia
PO Box 318 334, West Harbour, Auckland 0661 New Zealand
arkhousepress.com

Cataloguing in Publication Data:
Title: Grit, Grace and Hustle
ISBN: 978-0-6489194-7-6 (pbk)
Subjects: Business; Christian women;
Other Authors/Contributors: Reva, Rachel

Design by initiateagency.com

Email: rachel@rachelreva.com / support@lifeonherterms.com
Contact Details: 36 Tighe Street, Waratah 2298, New South Wales, Australia
Phone Number: +61426965384
Instagram: @instagram.com/lifeonherterms
FB: https://www.facebook.com/lifeonherterms/
Website: www.lifeonherterms.com

THIS BOOK IS DEDICATED TO:

My dear friend Alex, who continued to encourage me to keep writing this book over the past 7 years. Your friendship and loyalty mean the world to me.

To my mother Barbara, the kindest person I have ever known. The original writer in the family and the chief prayer warrior who points me to faith every day.

For my Grandmother Hazel. The southern cook. The story-teller. The song-writer and piano player who never had a lesson but if she heard the tune, could play the song. The Jesus-loving and church rearing mother who raised 7 children and bragged on her many grandchildren. The girl who wore red lipstick while working on the farm. Thank you for passing down your legacy of faith, humour and hustle. This book was only possible because of the grit and grace you displayed to all of us growing up. May your legacy long continue for the young women who come after us.

NOTICE TO THE READER:

References to Mr Hugh Grant have not been authorised by him or his representatives and he is not endorsing this book. The following stories which reference Mr Grant are factual accountings and recollections of an event that happened around the time of August 2014.

Contents

Introduction:
The Mega Star and the
Georgia Peach

"Rachel, Hugh Grant is going to be in your interview."

I spun around in my chair and stared at my colleague. *"Really?"*

"Yeah, just wanted to give you a heads up."

I nodded and smiled. *"No worries!"*

I turned around and tried to pick up where I left off on my computer—a blog about press intrusion. Important stuff! More important than meeting—and being interviewed by—a mega-celebrity. But inside, I was in total freak out mode.

I was new to the team—heck, new to the country—and wanted to play it cool. I had moved from Sydney to London only two months ago and, somehow, through God's divine provision and humour, ended up working for this cool group of campaigners, legislators, journalists, and lawyers—all of whom were exquisitely British. We were fighting for change to press legislation due to hacking scandals that had rocked the UK and the world only a few years prior. Actor and mega star Hugh Grant had been one of the victims and decided to help by being on the board of this not-for-profit organisation.

But I had thought that would be the extent of my involvement with Mr Grant. Maybe he'd come in for some private events or meetings, but I was only working on a temporary basis for the team. A full-time PR position had become available and I was being interviewed for it. This would be my second interview and, this time, Mr Grant would be on the panel.

Being the professional I was, all I could think was, *"What do I wear??"*

My boyfriend couldn't believe it.

"You've been in the country eight weeks."

"Yes."

"And you're going to be interviewed by a famous movie star?"

"It seems that way."

"It could only happen to you, Rachel."

I smiled. I knew what he meant. From an outsider's perspective, it looked as though things just 'worked out' for me. That, somehow, I was just one of the lucky ones.

This assumption couldn't be further from the truth.

I grew up in a trailer in Milledgeville, Georgia. I shared a bed with my little sister—the bottom bunk—while my older sister got the top to herself. My parents worked hard; we pretty much lived paycheck to paycheck. Every trip to the grocery store involved cutting coupons and buying anything we could in bulk. My mama also was known to cook for others, those who had less than we did, and it wasn't unusual to wake up and find someone sleeping on our couch. When I'd enquire about our guest, I'd hear the same response: *"They just needed a place to stay tonight."*

And here I was in London, twenty-five years later, about to be interviewed by a very famous person. I daydreamed, of course: me, this Georgia peach PR manager, meeting the British megastar who campaigned tirelessly for press regulation. He'd be so impressed with me. My southern charm, my cultured conversations, my Aussie references, my diverse experience living in different countries—he may even invite me to work on his team!

Clearly, everything I had done was leading up to this moment. Volunteering at newspapers, radio stations, and TV networks. Working at Kmart while my friends were vacationing in Bali and doing work experience everywhere I could get it. Whether it was working in health care PR or TV publicity, I wanted to make it. To succeed. To create a career and lifestyle on my terms.

I prayed. I read my Bible. I put my hand up for every opportunity in front of me. I watched nearly every Oprah episode, darn it! I could do this!

That's when my thoughts started to swirl from dream to shame.

"Who are you to do this? You don't have anything to offer here—you'll just sound like a cute redneck who got very lucky. You aren't special. You don't have enough experience to even step into that room... you're too American! Too Australian! Too un-British!"

Ever had one of those self-sabotage moments?

I call this person *Rude Rachel*. Yep, she has a name, because if you can't name it, you can't deal with the ridiculous thoughts and dismiss them. When *Rude Rachel* shows up, *Awesome Rachel* has to step up and say, *"Screw you, Rude Rachel! I can do this!"*

Yes, I can. And I did (more on that later).

But you didn't pick up this book because I met Hugh Grant (or maybe you saw his name and thought it would be a tell-all on Mr Grant. I'm afraid to disappoint you). While it makes for a fun story, the reason I even bring it up is because I hustled hard to make that moment happen.

The opportunities that came my way: offers to work for the biggest broadcaster in Australia, to move to London, to land my dream job at the BBC, to meet my dream guy and marry him, to be offered a sponsored visa role when everyone said it would be impossible, to start my own business....

I was delighted to get these opportunities, but frankly, I was never surprised.

Fortune favours the bold and the *kind*. Success comes to those who show some grit, hustle with heart, and extend grace to those behind them as they climb.

While I didn't have a roadmap for my career, I always had a vision. Of more: more influence, impact, money, travel, independence, giving back, serving, showing up as the best me, learning my craft, and being the go-to expert in my field.

I didn't just believe these things would happen for me; I worked as though they already were. I didn't just sit and wait for opportunities. I expected them while working purposefully.

You picked up this book because there is something in you that says you are ready for more. You deserve more, but are tired of doing it someone else's way. You want to succeed and be YOU, but feel exhausted acting like someone else at work. You breathe a sigh of relief every day when you get home, clock off or wine with your girlfriends, and can finally just be yourself.

For years, I was trained that I had to 'act like a man' to get ahead. And the women I saw in the top spots at work were either aggressive bullies or so passive that their roles had little to no influence. And I'm not here to criticise. Men invented the rules of the workplace—of course, it's going to be challenging for women to climb that ladder with class, grace, and authenticity.

But it's possible.

It's not only possible, but necessary.

I didn't think a girl from small town Georgia would ever be taken seriously—in news, in TV, in health—but I've met and rubbed shoulders with politicians, prime ministers, TV hosts, journalists and experts. I sounded different, looked different, talked about Oprah and Tony Robbins. I was a faith girl and came from a very humble background.

I wanted to do an outstanding job, but I was like a fish out of water in nearly every meeting, photo shoot, and event I attended.

Who was I to be there? To influence? To question? To challenge? To grow?

The answer is simple: Who was I NOT to do these things? And maybe… just maybe I was brought here for such a time as this. Maybe my oddball background, this American/Aussie girl, was exactly what was required in this moment to do the work that needed to be done—to cut through, show a different perspective.

After a while—and some major learning on the way—instead of trying to hide my 'southern' ways that were so inherently part of my personality, I embraced them. I showcased them.

This book is exactly that. It's about embracing and showcasing the brilliant you—the real you—that keeps a part hidden at work and in business because you're afraid of not being respected. Of being rejected. Of being seen less than worthy.

Well, sister, the time of hiding is over.

The time of acting your way through the day is done.

ENOUGH pretending to be someone else's version of success.

I'm here to remind you—to show you—it's YOUR time to shine. This life is your movie and YOU are the star, so stop playing in the background.

This book is a guide to get you back to the authentic YOU: how to show up with your truth, to ask for anything and everything you truly want, to take confident action and create a life and career that represents REAL success for you.

Meeting a mega celebrity isn't the answer.

You are the mega celebrity, and it's time to take front and centre in your very own life and career. Because God has some incredible plans laid out for you. You were created for IMPACT. For AWESOME. For something so particular, so specific and bespoke— tailored for your personality, your likes, your dislikes, your experience, your background, your hurts, your mistakes. It's all a recipe that's going to help propel you exactly where you were designed to be.

So get ready to show up with fearless authenticity and say YES to everything God has waiting for you. We can't wait to meet you on the other side.

And ACTION....

CHAPTER 1

Goodbye people pleasing, hello freedom

"If there's one thing I'm willing to bet on, it's myself"
—Beyoncé

I wrote this book when I was on the verge of leaving my TV career. Little did I know that I would be soon starting my own business, which required a different type of hustle and a whole lot more grace.

Looking back, I so wish I had seen a similar book when I was starting out in my own career. As a spiritual gal who genuinely tried to put others first and had a heart for people, I was so easily stomped on, overlooked, and seen as 'too nice' for too long.

My niceness was holding me back. Or so I thought.

What had really been holding me back was people pleasing. And not being totally upfront, clear, and unapologetic about what I wanted. Saying yes to everything, waiting to be asked by management to join a project, waiting to be seen for what I really deserved, financially and position wise.

Being a nice person wasn't the problem (and don't delude yourself into thinking not nice people are the only ones to catch the breaks). My issue was being passive, silent, and allowing myself to shrink in the background when I knew I was meant for more.

Nice girls CAN get the corner office. Your manners and heart for people can be your greatest superpower, once trained and pointed in the right direction.

As women, we have such incredible opportunities like never before to rise up, take a stand for our vision and make our lives the incredible success we deserve and desire.

On the back of the #metoo campaign we have seen a rally cry. It's about equality, but it's more than that. It's about women speaking their truth.

It took me a while to learn how to speak my truth in my own career, and even in my relationships. I'm here to make sure you learn the tools, strategies and realities behind what it takes to be a *real* success when you are a kind person, have faith and genuinely want to help people as you climb the ladder.

I grew up in a Christian home and saw incredible women doing incredible things in the mission field, in the church and with their families. But when it came to navigating my own career, I felt like a loner. I couldn't see any female mentors in the TV environment I was working in. I desperately wanted to succeed in my career, but I wanted to do it the right way. I didn't want to experience someone else's version of success.

What I discovered is that I was taught two ways to be successful as a woman: be the nice girl or be the aggressive bully. I couldn't find an in-between.

So, I created my own. And found out that YES, you can be successful by being you. The authentic, here I am, REAL you.

No, you don't have to be a bully to get what you want. And you don't have to be the nice girl who just smiles and agrees with everyone else.

But you will have to take action that makes you a little uncomfortable at times—anything that will make you grow will do that. You have to know that, no matter what's going on in your life, that it's happening for you, not to you. You have to be certain that God's got your back, that you ARE the Plan B and—no matter what's thrown at you—you can handle it.

Not just handle it—you can OWN it.

This book is my guide, my secret little black book that will show you how to be yourself, communicate with confidence, have difficult conversations and live out the success you desire to have in your life and career.

You can succeed by being yourself. Forget what others have said.

Yes, there are some guidelines to follow. But this book is about empowering you to follow your intuition, hustle your heart out, and have grace for others. When you do this, it's my experience and belief that success does follow.

It's spiritual principle and universal law.

You just gotta adapt a little. And lead with grace and move with hustle.

Manners are free, first impressions are expensive

It's really hard being nice to people in your life all the time.

At least, it is for me. It's easy when you're having a good day and everyone's getting along in life: the train came on time for work, you didn't have to wait in line for a coffee, that deadline was met with ease and your new boss remembered your name. But some days—when I'm running late, deadlines are creeping (or passed), and people seem to be ignoring my phone calls or emails when I'm trying to get an urgent answer to a question—I struggle to have a Doris Day attitude.

I know I'm not the only one. I have many times been on the other side of someone's bad day and it amazes me how commonplace being rude actually is.

After seven years of working in television, I have seen the ups and downs of working with 'talented people.' Whether it be television or film stars, journalists, or politicians, I have first-hand of experience of what success can do to people.

They forget to be NICE. I find it incredible how the most basic concepts of human connection, compassion, and politeness escape certain people. Not just once, or on an odd occasion, but constantly. And it isn't just people on the screen. Journalists who want to get a story, producers who assume their job is more important than anything else and do anything to get publicity: bullying, harassing, you name it.

In the entertainment industry, there is a considerable amount of pressure people are under. While we may enjoy watching a certain tv show now and then, on the other side of the screen are actors, producers, studio crew members, directors and networks that are relying on you to watch that program above anything else available. Their income depends on it. Most contracts are anywhere from three to six months; if a program's a flop, they're back to the drawing board for employment. It's an adventurous—sometimes cruel—industry. Daily deadlines, public scrutiny, press reviews, landing a story—these are the things a publicist deals with on a daily basis.

It's a completely different world compared to the 9-5 business, so let's be honest and say we can't expect angelic behaviour all the time. But it got to a point where it was unreasonable for me to expect civility from most of the people I came across. I can count on one hand the amount of truly 'nice' people I have dealt with in my career. It's rather disappointing.

Why this book?

One day, I met a presenter who I organised a photo shoot for and he was quite pleasant to deal with. He was well known, successful, starting a respected position and had no dues to pay. He had no one to impress. Usually people in his position—a seasoned journalist who has been around the block—has a certain attitude. They're not used to waiting for more than five minutes for anything; it's accepted that they don't have time to spare and an arrogant attitude is, well… normal. This time was different.

It was an easy photo shoot; I have managed many like it before. It was nothing special or particularly difficult, just head shots for the website or press stories. Afterwards, he sent me an email just to say thank you for organising the shoot, that it all ran smoothly, and he looked forward to working with me in the future.

It was short, kind, and incredibly effective. My reaction was—some would say—a little over the top. Everyone in my department heard about this email and how 'wonderful' this person was and how delightful it was to work with him. I couldn't believe how this one gesture affected me and my view of this person so profoundly. After that, he had (and still has) a fan for life. I would happily go the extra mile for this presenter because he showed me kindness and respect that is, unfortunately, very rare in the television industry. It dawned on me: I couldn't remember the last time I had been sent an unprompted thank you from a presenter, or anyone else at work.

If we truly know everything there is to know about success, about achieving everything you want in your life and career, then why are people so miserable?

Niceness and kindness are nice clichés on social media, yet so rarely practiced in the workplace. People are more stressed out then ever, climbing over each other to get to the 'top' so they get to the elusive Nirvana: enjoy success and be happy (on a beach, with a laptop, taking selfies).

Divorce is up, family time is down and people are working longer hours. We replace our relationships with likes and a text on the way to get our morning coffee. This is the way we 'connect' as human beings.

What's changed? We've forgotten about real connection. To care about others. To lead with heart. To extend grace.

The Oxford dictionary defines nice as *"giving pleasure or satisfaction; pleasant or attractive."* Other definitions include: *pleasing; agreeable; delightful, amiably pleasant; kind, characterized by, showing, or requiring great accuracy, precision, skill, tact, care, or delicacy, refined in manners.*

What a compliment if the only one thing people can say about you is that you are a nice person? What's wrong with doing something well and with kindness and dignity?

This book will show you how to live a 'nice' life and give you examples of people who made it with graciousness and dignity and succeeded. It's the old adage that manners will take you where money can't. In my own career, I have seen the ripple effect kindness has.

It has given me an edge. Seriously.

John Maxwell wrote *The Difference Maker,* a motivational book about how your attitude towards work and life will stand out and often trump experience, connections and a glossy CV. The way we treat others, and think about life in general, has a way of standing out.

It also goes the other way.

It's very hard to undo the work of someone who has treated you unkindly. Think about the last person who you felt treated you badly. It could have been a waitress at your local coffee shop or someone you work with. How hard is it for you to change your mind about that person? It's not an easy order.

It's also not easy being nice to everyone 100 percent of the time—I'm anything but perfect! And, in the end, it's not about perfection. It's about progress.

You picked up this book because something stood out to you: you want to improve an area of your life, empower yourself, and learn some strategies that will take you to the next level.

Go you!

This book is a reminder of how niceness is so rare in the world we live in, yet so effective. Lead with grace and kindness and it will change the way people perceive you, or just improve your already awesome reputation.

What's the difference between this and other books? It's a call to action. Not for world peace, but in your life. To your loved ones, the people you work with, your neighbours or locals at a bus station.

I come from a small town in Georgia. I lived there until I was fourteen, when my family and I moved to Australia—definitely a change of scenery! While I've been a city girl for nearly a decade, I still have deep within me some southern principles that I hope I'll retain forever. In fact, they were the inspiration for this book.

Southern hospitality is known for being welcoming, friendly and genuine. I spent a great deal of my childhood growing up in Georgia and know some of these principles are still relevant today. I use them. Don't get me wrong, I can still use some reminding every now and then, but these are rules for life. We all think we're 'nice' people, but there is always room for improvement.

Want to get ahead at work? Introduce yourself to someone you have never met. Want to improve your relationship with your spouse or sibling? Organise something special just for them. Want to be happier? Start looking at ways you can be nicer in your community. Volunteer at a homeless shelter, help with a fundraiser, or just pick up trash around your local park. Little things change everything.

I use my southern principles that are simple, truthful, and time tested for success. What is it about the south? The people are genuine and welcoming (in that order), and every person truly matters. People are happy to help others without question of anything in return.

New York Times short story author George Saunders gave a speech to the graduating class of Syracuse University in 2013. Failures of kindness, he said, was the biggest regret of his life:

"What I regret most in my life are failures of kindness. Those moments when another human being was there, in front of me, suffering, and I responded … sensibly. Reservedly. Mildly. Or, to look at it from the other end of the telescope: Who, in your life, do you remember most fondly, with the most undeniable feelings of warmth? Those who were kindest to you, I bet. It's a little facile, maybe, and certainly hard to implement, but I'd say, as a goal in life, you could do worse than: Try to be kinder."

Saunders' simple words struck a powerful nerve. Within hours of the graduating ceremony, it went viral on the internet. Random House has since struck him a book deal.

It's a powerful thing. More powerful than people realise. Above all else, I would rather be known for being kind and nice than being good at my profession, a team player, or the first to work in the morning.

If I am truly a kind and nice person, the world around me is affected for the better and so am I.

As humans, we all really want the same thing: to be noticed, acknowledged, and loved (even that grumpy neighbour who complains about everything). Everyone wants this. In a world that preaches the only important thing is 'me, me, me'—that you should do what makes YOU happy and take care of yourself first—it doesn't work, except to perpetuate the narcissistic culture we seem to find ourselves in.

The fact that you picked up this book shows that you know there's more to life than just meeting your own needs—you want to succeed and help others along the way. You want to make it to the top, but not because you kicked someone out or had to pretend to be someone else to make it in those circles. You want to live out the destiny you were created for and experience success that actually makes you smile, not live in anxious freak out mode because you're wasting energy acting like the person you think everyone wants you to be.

It's about using the gifts you've been given and showing up, even when your hands are shaking. Asking for that meeting, even when you aren't 100% sure what the outcome will be, or putting your hand up for that project because it makes you both nervous and excited.

It's about going for that promotion before you feel ready. Using your voice and speaking your truth with confidence. Lifting as you climb, and encouraging as you challenge.

It's time to take action, empower yourself and start creating the success that you deserve to have.

Exercise: Who is the kindest person you know? What makes them kind? What actions or characteristics do they have that you admire? Write these down. Think about the last time you showed these yourself.

CHAPTER 2

Myths about what works

"What makes you different or weird, that's your strength"
—Meryl Streep

B efore we start, I want to get real about the myths I believed for way too long when I was first starting out in my career. Let's just get these out in the open, because I know some of you may be hearing these outdated ideas behind 'what it takes' to get what you want.

Please note: the version of success I talk about in this book isn't some hack that promises *"you can go from the reception desk to running a company in six months' time."* While I love to dream big, I'm a big believer in the long game: show up, smile, do your job exceptionally well, always look where you can add value. Be approachable, be teachable, and be open to what doors may open up along the way.

And, most importantly, allow yourself time to grow.

Real things take time. And right now, it's time to get real about what strategies don't work in the long term when you're creating success for yourself. Anyone can talk themselves into a cool job, but to build yourself a career and reputation that is lasting, that feels good to you—let that be the goal.

Maya Angelou said: *"My mission in life is not merely to survive, but to thrive; and to do so with some passion, some compassion, some humour, and some style. Success is liking yourself, liking what you do, and liking how you do it."* Amen to that!

Myth 1: To get ahead, you have to smarter, brasher, louder.

This may work in the short term. In fact, it will almost always work straight away.

When you yell the loudest and demand the most, people will jump quickly just to shut you up. You'll get a reaction, but you will also get a reputation. In retail, there was always *that* customer. The one who demanded a refund, even when our policy clearly stated they were not possible. Management reacted quickly to these customers, because they wanted to get them out the door—and they did.

There was always a repercussion to this: there would be a new policy, or a note about certain customers—do not sell this item to this customer, or make them sign a waiver and keep it on file. We would go the extra mile to ensure this customer would not get their way again or have reason to complain. And when they came back to the store? I wasn't too keen on helping them.

Now, the 'nice' customers... you know, the ones who don't bark when they have to wait for five minutes and don't threaten employees when their kid doesn't get the toy they wanted for Christmas? The ones who say please and thank you and 'take your time' and 'have a good day'? I would go to heaven and beyond.

I would bend the rules a little because I wanted their business and their nice attitude in the store. When you're a nice person with nice intentions and manners to back them up, you'll find yourself ahead of the pack.

Stanford University's Graduate School of Business published "The Psychology of Kindness in the Workplace," in which scholars explain how a culture of caring and compassion is necessary at work. For example, forgiving a worker's mistake is perceived by others as good leadership. If you wish to move up to a leadership position, being harsh with others may hold you back.

My point is this: listen to the Brits. Keep calm.

Myth 2: Nice guys finish last.

Nice guys may finish 'later' than others, but only because a reputation will take some time to catch up with you. But it will. We reap what we sow.

Throughout this book, you will see real life examples of nice people winning in life and their kindness is no coincidence. It's a reason for their success. Not the ONLY reason, mind you. I am not diluted enough to suggest being nice without hard work will get you anywhere. It will help though. Manners will always take you where money can't. Being 'nice' also doesn't mean being a pushover—you can be polite but still have boundaries.

It's possible and, later on, I will show you how to keep your boundaries and cool intact.

My point? Nice will win in the long run. Don't sacrifice your gentle self for your ego.

Myth 3: There's no point in being nice to people. It makes no difference as long as you do your job right.

We are social creatures, even the introverted ones. Unfortunately, your job competency is not as important as how you get along with your team and how management 'views' you.

We know this, but statistics back it up: if you are liked, you are more likely to be considered for promotion or for big projects.

A recent survey by Right Now show that 86 per cent of people are willing to pay for better customer service. Managers would rather hire someone 'likeable' and who is a team player they can train than an expert who alienates people. People are the most important part of any job you are in.

Sometimes this does mean that the 'players' who are very good at the social game will do well, while perhaps not completing their KPI's so well. People crave to feel like they matter—it's the most basic human need we all have.

You are different. If you do your job well, and continually strive to be kind and polite in the process, these two combinations will make you an appealing employee choice and an unstoppable success.

The point is that talent alone won't get you where you want to be. Focus on people and serving.

CHAPTER

3

Know what you're aiming for

*"I figure if a girl wants to be a legend, she
should just go ahead and be one"*
—Calamity Jane

I always knew, instinctively, that I wanted to build a career for myself in the media field. I went to university, got as much work experience as I could and worked my butt off while my friends were vacationing in Bali so I could quickly get to where I wanted.

Where did I want to be? The top. That was it. I wanted to manage a team, have influence, make decisions, and be excellent at my craft.

I was relentless in pursuing work experience and internship opportunities because I knew holding a degree in communications would only get me so far. And I was right. You'll later see the breaks I was working for had more to do with showing up—and HOW I showed up. I landed my first full-time job just because I was doing an internship in a team, and a lady I had barely said two words to ended up being my reference. She told my manager I should be hired because *"I seemed like a nice girl."*

I always wanted the next step, and within six months of landing a job I had a timeline of how long I would be staying in a certain role. Life is short, you are awesome, and time is precious. Make sure you have a clear vision of what you want. That vision should be both short-term and long-term. Know where you want to be in five years, and know how where you are now will help you get there.

What's your vision for your career? Why did you buy this book? I wanted to succeed, to make great money, to love my work, and work with programs that produced award-winning content. My vision would later change as my desires changed *(hint: allow yourself the room to do this)*, but the vision of MORE was always there.

'Without a vision, people perish' (Proverbs 29.18)

If you don't have a vision, you'll be working for someone else's.

God has given you a desire in your heart. It could look like a corner office, opening an orphanage, starting your own business, working with horses, starting a podcast, travelling the world—the possibilities are endless. I don't believe we dream up things; I believe that God gives us dreams as glimpses into what He has for us.

A glimpse into what is possible.

Sometimes a glimpse is all you need to get you started in one direction. So, even if you don't have that clarity yet, you need a vision to help you think bigger. Right now, I have a Pinterest board called "Rachel's awesome life," where I collect images of the beach house I've been dreaming about for years. I see it every day and am literally reminding myself that this particular vision is coming.

It needs to be that powerful for you.

In my career, I didn't allow myself thoughts of anything but success. As Oprah says, *"What we dwell on we become."* I knew to get what I wanted in my life so I had to become that person. I'll be sharing with you some time-tested strategies, experiences (and good ol' common sense) that has helped my build the career I desired for myself—authentically.

But first? Get that vision sparkling like Dolly Parton's handbag and make it feel real.

Exercise: What's the next level for you? Get clear on this, close your eyes for 5 minutes and ask yourself: What do I really want from my career? Who do I want to become? What do I want to achieve? How do I want to spend my days? How much money do I want to make? How can I show up more with my gifts in a joyful way? What would my PERFECT Monday look like? That's your vision. Record it – journal it, Pinterest it, sing it, vision board it, tape it to your bathroom mirror, put it on your phone – just make sure it's visible to you – somewhere. Without a vision, you will never achieve what you really desire and your dreams will die. Know what your goal is, remind yourself EVERY single day of this vision and you'll get there quicker and save a lot of time for yourself.

CHAPTER 4

Please, after you and thank you

"Strong women fight with grace in their heart, kindness in their voice and love on their soul"
—Hannah Elaine

Let's start with basics. This sounds SO simple. Of course, every kid is taught that right? You say *"please"* and *"thank you"* and don't cut in line. Pleasantries travel with the person where they go; whether it be the grocery store, church, the guy on the street or dinner at the golf club, you treat people with respect. Even when a person rubs you the wrong way, pleasantries such as *"please"* and *"thank you"* are not disregarded.

I worked as a television publicist for seven years. In my job, I worked with tv presenters, producers, and actors. Some could be so charming; it was hard not to be incredibly smitten with their attention. But there was one thing they couldn't hide: a truly nice and humble person treats everyone they come across equally.

Sadly, that usually wasn't the case.

I noticed instantly if they snapped at the waiter, or how they treated their concierge or wardrobe stylist. It's hard to ignore how someone speaks to their spouse or child on the phone. They might be sweet as pie to the publicist (because I'm the one booking the interviews and dealing with journalists) but some will only make small talk or acknowledge another person if they are deemed 'worthy' of speaking to.

I became an expert at identifying these fake traits.

Funnily enough, it's usually actors or presenters who were raised in small towns that seem to take the cake in the nice categories. Hold on, city folk—I'm not talking trash you! It's just an observation. City folk can be mighty pleasant and kind, but it's harder to come by; because everyone in the city is in a rush, *manners seem to be a luxury now-a-days.*

I know this from personal experience. I have seen the most beautiful people turn hideous before my eyes, simply because their ego was bigger than anything else in the room—definitely too big to treat the TV crew or publicist with respect. Oh, they'll turn it on for the cameras (read: paycheck) or for fans (read: ego serving), but no one else matters.

I do believe being 'nice' and 'kind' will change your outward appearance to people. I have seen men that aren't anything to write home about. But after a gentlemanly gesture, say... helping an older lady cross the street? Well, they may as well be Ryan Gosling in my book. That's an attractive man. Manners will get you where money won't.

Kate Reardon is the editor of *Tatler*, an magazine published in the UK that focuses on fashion, lifestyle and high society. In a speech to a group of high school graduates, she said: *"It doesn't matter how many A levels you have, what kind of degree... if you have good manners people will like you. And if people like you they will help you. I'm talking about being polite and respectful and making people feel valued."*

I am a living example of this truth. I have never been the smartest or the quickest. But I would work my butt off, say yes to everything that came my way and do it with a smile. People helped me because I genuinely tried to help them first.

Think about it.

CHAPTER 5

Frankly, my dear, I don't give a darn

*"Greatness is hearing your truth and speaking it,
no matter how your voice shakes"*
—Mel Robbins

Gone with the Wind is one of the most popular films in cinematic history and was the highest grossing film until *Titanic* came along. The love story, set amongst the Civil war, with Scarlett O'Hara and the rogue Rhett Butler has captured the imagination of many over the years.

At the end of the film (SPOILER ALERT), Rhett has finally had enough of Scarlett. For many reasons—I could spend a lot of time rehashing this story, but let's just say he's done with the relationship. Which is right when Scarlett realises that Rhett was the best thing that ever happened to her, and that she really did love him.

When she sees the love of her life leaving, she begs him to stay. He is completely unmoved and turning to leave when she cries, *"But Rhett... Where will I go? What will I do?"*

Rhett delivers one of the coolest lines ever spoken: *"Frankly, my dear, I don't give a da*n."* And he walks away. The relationship is over. For the first time in her life, Scarlett is left to fend for herself.

Props to Rhett for his handling of this dramatic situation.

Why do I love this line? And why is it relevant in a book about being successful? Well, the answer is simple: because Rhett got his point across effectively and nicely. He was kind but firm. He was committed to his decision—he had had enough and was ready to leave his wife—but he was still a southern gentleman. He could have gone on a tirade about how pathetic she was, counting all the times she wasn't there for him, about how she was unworthy of his love and devotion, but he simply said one sentence, put his hat on and went on his way. He was firm but kind. *Firm but kind.* He didn't embarrass or humiliate her, but he made his point clear.

I want to be like Rhett Butler in every unfair, frustrating and unjust situation.

Let me be clear about the intention here. **Being nice does not mean being a pushover.** It means *not* embarrassing, humiliating or taking advantage of people (even if they deserve it). This is a hard one.

Sometimes the cards are so in our favour—the evidence is on the wall of how someone has wronged us—and yet we don't need to lower our standard of attitude. Nice can be enough. No matter how badly people treat you, never drop down to their level. Just know that you're bigger than that and walk away. Remember you reap what you sow.

I know I've had some 'grace' moments early in my career with people when I have made mistakes—not intentionally, but just learning the ropes—and I have had the grace of being on the end of these 'nice moments.' It's only in being on the receiving end that you realise how powerful it is to show restraint when you have been wronged or when someone has really messed up. It is a powerful gesture that would not be forgotten quickly.

Somewhere along the way, us gals got it in our heads that being a 'good girl' means being okay when someone at work makes inappropriate comments, or keeping our mouth shut when we are overlooked or when someone is perpetually late and disrespecting our time. As a woman, you need to let your YES be a YES and NO be a NO.

How is this relevant at work and at home?

You can actually say 'no' to that extra work that somehow always ends up on your desk NICELY without complaining, making it clear what your work boundaries are. That passive aggressive colleague who keeps testing you? You can be perfectly nice and professional by saying, *"No, I don't have time for that, I'm afraid,"* or *"I would like to help you, but I'm afraid it isn't possible for me to do so at this time."*

Manipulative people LOVE nice people who can't say no. They can sniff you out at the coffee cart pretty quickly and know just what to say to get you bending over backwards doing things for them that are outside your job description—repeatedly.

They know if they can give you a sob story, you'll pick up whatever they are struggling with and not breathe a word about it. They are experts at making their issues your issues.

This isn't about dismissing being a team player. It's about recognising when you are going from supporting a colleague to being used by a co-worker.

We all have personal boundaries. You can say you are a relaxed person, but I can assure you there is something you would not be okay with. This could be a hug from someone you first met, or a friend dropping by unannounced, or a colleague leaving their things on your desk repeatedly.

We all have our things and that's perfectly okay.

However, it is *your* responsibility to define those boundaries by speaking out and teaching other people how to treat you—how can they be expected to know unless they are informed?

How do you know if one of your boundaries are being violated? You feel it—it's a gut feeling you get when something is asked or required of you (and it's not a nice one). This is when you are aware there is a boundary perhaps being crossed here.

All you need to say is this: *"I don't feel comfortable with this."* Or, *"Let me have a think and I'll get back to you."* That's it.

When a relative who owes you a lot of money asks for more, you can simply say, *"Sorry. I can't right now."* That person at work who has been an absolute nightmare and owes you about twenty apologies? Not worth waiting on, but when that person approaches you again (or you have to work with them), you can communicate kindly and effectively what you find inappropriate and how you would like to work together (i.e. be treated) in the future.

It doesn't need to be a long poem or excuse diatribe. You don't need to explain your reasons to anyone (except maybe your manager, who you can approach with facts and a reasonable conversation).

People can't argue with your feelings but they can argue at how you express them.

I know a colleague who felt such guilt if she didn't say yes to every request that came across her desk at work. She would send long emails, have torturous phone calls explaining herself and begging for sympathy when the outcome of the situation was the same regardless: she couldn't help. Yet she spent more time, energy, and emotional labour in these situations that would have been better left with a clear *"Would love to help, but I can't."* This is not 'passing the bucket'; it's called having boundaries and communicating them clearly and effectively. If you try to please everyone, you will end up miserable.

Annie Lamont said *"No is a complete sentence."* The word 'no' will give you so much freedom.

Where possible, if someone comes to your desk to ask you to do something (and they aren't your manager), always ask them to email you. This way, you can send a politely-worded email to respond with your answer (and check in with your manager where appropriate). Trust me, when someone sees you going down the formal route, you won't get as many requests outside your normal job requirements, leaving you to focus on the job at hand.

Less is more and is usually a nicer and better way to communicate.

Please note: this isn't about passing the bucket or ignoring projects that can help you stand out and achieve more at work. It's about having boundaries and not getting sucked into other people's drama at work—I speak from experience!

Asking for a raise with class

I've also used this strategy when asking for a raise. I have asked for a salary increase in nearly every role I've had. Some requests were successful, some not, but I would always ask the question (at the appropriate time, of course, such as a job performance review, a manager coming back from maternity leave when I have stepped up, or when a certain achievement has been made).

As a woman, it is important to ask for what you believe you are worth—and what is doable for your organisation. Asking for more is not 'testing fate'; if done in a professional setting with evidence to back up your request (and manners, of course), there is no reason why a manager wouldn't consider your request.

Even if more money isn't on the table, I can guarantee you it puts you in a position of power. Your manager will look at you and ask, *"How else can we reward this person?"*

It will also be very telling of your value to the company and whether you have a foreseeable future there. It's a shortcut to know what your manager thinks about you. If they bend over backwards to keep you or make you happy, even if a raise isn't possible that quarter, you'll know they see you as an investment. If not—if they just say, *"Sorry, but it's not possible. Keep doing your job"*—I would start looking at my next professional step.

You need to be able to take your emotions out of such a conversation. Remember that every negotiation starts with the Rhett Butler attitude: approaching the issue politely and in confidence of what you bring to the table. It's the classy way to get ahead.

CHAPTER
6

Don't get too big for your britches

"Stay hungry and humble"
—Quincy Jones

Be humble. No one is perfect, including you.

I've dealt with many types of 'talent,' but two actors stand out in my mind. A particular actor—let's call him Al—who has well known in Australia in the 80s was starring in a new tele-movie. I wasn't aware of his past work, but was asked to take him to some television interviews one week by another colleague. I had the time and was happy to do so.

On this particular morning, we had to be at an interview at 8.00am. I was told to arrive at his address at a given time and to call upon arrival. I arrived, but he was nowhere to be seen. I called; he didn't answer. He actually left me waiting in a cab for half an hour, the meter still running. When he finally did mosey out from his apartment, he seemed unperturbed by the fact the meter was already up to $70 when he got in the cab.

Not only did he fail to pick up his phone to say, *"I'm running late,"* but he said his alarm was broken and he had a big night the night before. I had to bite my tongue and I did; I knew it would make no difference at this point. The cab ride was fine, as long as we spoke about him and his likes and his life. I found out a lot about his family, his home, his music tastes.

I found his demeanour ungracious and arrogant, but I thought maybe this is just a rare day for him.

Two days later, we met again. This time, we were to meet at a studio for another interview. Again, he was late. I called him to see how far away he was from the studio (we had other actors, a tv crew, and the host all sitting waiting on him to arrive). He snapped at me because he couldn't find the car park.

When he finally arrived, he was stressed out and brought the whole mood down of the crew. He had a financial issue and decided everyone should know about it—it was obvious he just wanted in and out. One of the older actors who had arrived early, was polite and waiting for this actor to arrive made the comment: *"I'm old school, I arrive on time. He arrives when it suits him."* He wasn't impressed.

I remember thinking, *"He's saying this to me, what would he say to others about him?"* This guy thought his reputation was more important than having basic manners, such as apologising for holding up an entire crew, keeping someone waiting outside for thirty minutes and being late.

I couldn't believe how he treated people—and how he assumed it was okay because of his 'status.' I had no idea who he was, but will always remember him as *that guy* who made my job really hard and unenjoyable for two days. When his name is brought up, I have to bite my tongue. Really hard.

On the flip side, I've met people who have made my work enjoyable. This does not mean 'clear sailing,' but they decided to bring a 'nice' approach when working with others.

Another former high school star from a daily soap opera in the 80s was exactly the opposite. I again had no idea of this man's profile until I filled in as his publicist while he was in Sydney for interviews.

He was a charmer. Incredibly fun, he enjoyed his work because he didn't take it too seriously, and was a popular icon in the Australian media. I was very aware that he was a 'people person' and had this uncanny ability to make every person he spoke to feel like they were the most important person in the world. It was a lovely change from what I was usually dealing with on a daily basis: chasing facts, hunting down producers for information, and writing media alerts. I noticed I hadn't heard anyone say one bad thing about him, but I thought it best to hold my judgement until I worked with him myself.

We had a few very good days meeting with journalists and I saw how much effort he put into every interview and the person conducting it. He smiled, asked questions, and worked hard to connect with every person he was in the room with.

It was hard not to be smitten.

One day, he too was running late for an interview. I called to check on him; he was not in a good way. The car that the network had organised hadn't arrived so, understandably, he was stressed. He couldn't get a cab and he was running late for this particular interview.

He ranted at me for about five minutes. He said he couldn't believe how he was being treated; he had tried so hard for this series and we couldn't even get him a car on time. He had what we call a 'mini-melt down'.

I listened, assured him that everything would be fine and apologised on behalf of my team. When I got off the phone, I was disappointed but I knew he had a bad morning—haven't we all? I nervously awaited his arrival, not sure what mood to expect when he did.

When he finally did arrive, he apologised and gave me a hug. The charm was back on.

We grabbed a coffee and went into the interview and continued as though nothing had happened. I was thoroughly impressed with him. Why? He was humble enough to apologise for losing it—even if it was somewhat justified—and we could continue working and get the job done in a positive way. He's human. We all make mistakes. He was just humble enough to admit his.

That's a real pro. And a genuinely nice person.

CHAPTER

7

Mend the fences

"She remembered who she was and the game changed"
—Lalah Delias

I hate apologising. I don't believe I am alone in this.

Sadly, I find it easier to apologise to people I work with and eat 'humble pie' than with those who are closest to me. This could be because I think those at home will put up with more from me. Being wrong is not fun, but it's called being human. And yet, I find it appalling when someone is genuinely in the wrong but will tiptoe around the issue and say everything but an apology.

So, I am anything but righteous in this situation: I hate apologising and I also hate it when people refuse to. However, my detest of being wrong will not stop me apologising when I know someone is owed it. If you have worked with or been in a relationship long enough with someone, an apology will inevitably be deserved on each side. I also find—much like the band-aid method—the quicker you deal with it, the issue (and the person) heals quickly, usually with no scars left, and you can move on with your relationship.

I have a few examples of this, which I call my 'humble pie' section. I eat a lot of it, you see, and if this can help in any way your work, family or home relationships, I am glad to be of service.

Humble Pie for Phone Rudeness

One day I was rushing out the door for a work event. It was after 5pm. The phone rang and I assumed it was a presenter either asking details for this event or cancelling at the last minute, which tends to happen. Instead, it was a journalist. Not just any journalist—a tabloid journalist, calling from a particular publication that had been less than kind to my employer the last week.

In fact, it seemed to be an agenda item to print as much 'negative' coverage of our network as possible—including leaking the salary of the top paid presenters—which explains my less than ecstatic response when I heard, *"Hi, it's Nathan from News Limited."*

I immediately jumped on the defensive and said *"I'm heading out the door. What do you want?"* I was surprised at my own abruptness. It wasn't like me, but I was in a rush and frankly nervous about what this journalist wanted from me.

"Is there anyone else I can speak to?" he asked.

"Just tell me what you want." (This couldn't be ME talking, I thought. I'm usually so nice!)

"...I was just calling to see if there was an embargoed transcript of tonight's event announcement."

Whew. It was an easy one. He wouldn't be quoting me on a random news issue or asking for the statistics of staff redundancies or how many episodes of Lateline aired this year compared to the year before. It was a normal request (and he asked nicely). I told him it wasn't available and quickly got off the phone. I knew instantly I was rude to him and regretted my unnecessary manner.

A colleague overheard the conversation. *"Serves him right for calling after 5pm!"*

I ignored the feeling of guilt and rushed out the door. I'm ashamed to admit that I did not call him the next morning. In fact, I waited two days until I was reminded when a colleague mentioned his name and how he was a new journalist trying to make contacts. I knew my first impression would stick and I didn't want to be tarred with my 'rude' brush, which I so detested.

I called the guy three times until he picked up the phone, as I didn't want to just leave a message. He of course remembered me and I apologised for my rude manner. I said I really had no excuse but every phone call I had this week from a News Limited journalist was not a 'good' one. He laughed and said he understood and appreciated the phone call.

I bring this up because, well, I hate being wrong. But more than that? I feel that being rude to someone is a loss of self-control. It is weak and unnecessary.

Mending the fences is an important part of living a nice life. Being the first to apologise is difficult, but worth it in the long run. It shows that you are human and humble, and people do think better of you for it.

Humble Pie for Email Rudeness

As a publicist, your job is all about managing relationships and your reputation. Not unlike many other jobs, except sometimes you are dealing with actors, presenters, producers, and writers who can be quite 'definite' in their ideas, sensitive about feedback or disagreement, and fanatical about their own projects.

I get it. You live and die by your last project and, as a publicist, you have to 'show the love' as much as you can while prioritising every programme, film or request that comes in. Emails are the mode of communication we use when we want something on record and need a response from another party. I had a particularly bad run one month with a string of 'challenging' producers and was told very late to prioritise a last-minute program.

I resented it—I had too much on my plate at the time—but took it anyway. I soon met with the producers and director, who had very 'big' ideas for a documentary that, sadly, wasn't as ground-breaking as they imagined.

I tried to be diplomatic in my approach and was clear about the media I would be targeting, which is normal practice. I soon found out the director was taking matters into his own hands and contacting the media himself after I had started my own campaign. Instead of picking up the phone (hindsight is awesome), I composed a passionately worded essay and cced as many people as possible, stating my outrage and shock at his actions after we had discussed what I would be doing.

Was I justified? Yes, I actually was. Was it effective? No, it absolutely was not.

I had an equally 'passionate' email from the senior producer, who of course defended his director friend, and we weren't on friendly terms. I ended up calling him and we discussed in detail what had happened and the appropriateness of it. He agreed he would keep the director in line.

I mentioned I wasn't usually this aggressive in my approach

"*Yes,*" the producer said. "*I asked about you and people said this wasn't like you.*"

I felt sick in that moment. This wasn't like me. While I had a right to be angry and annoyed, I wasn't helping my reputation in emailing aggressive and passionate messages to colleagues and staff members.

What's the take home message here?

Edit and get a colleague to have a look before you press send on an emotive email. I now write my passionate emails, have a cup of tea, and come back to it an hour later. Responding in anger will only do harm, yet it's so easy to do in the world of instant communication we live in. Have a breather and even pick up the phone if you can.

In the long run, a nice conversation or a quick professional email will leave your reputation intact.

Even when it is deserved, being 'nice' will help in the long run.

I've also found baked goods to be a wonderful leveller when relationships are strained. It's difficult to think poorly of someone when they are offering you a homemade chocolate brownie. Think about it.

Humble Pie for Love Rudeness

The worst kind, yet most likely to happen. When I wrote this chapter, I was sitting in a hotel lobby at 11pm one evening. My boyfriend (now husband) was doing an interview for a job in the UK that he had been preparing for weeks on end. It had been a stressful time, to say the least. I had tried my best to be a supportive partner, but lately my 'grace levels' had not been where they should have been. I had stopped being nice to him and began barely tolerating him, thinking to myself, *"Dear God when will it end?"* It's an ugly side of me that ashamedly creeps up sometimes.

The funny thing is I know that if a colleague or close friend were in the same position my boyfriend was in, I would switch that attitude and put on my 'nice face'—the polite one that attempts to be fair, approachable, and helpful when possible, even as I'm gritting my teeth in frustration. Why can't I do the same to the people I love who are closest to me?

Why shouldn't I give a darn about being nice to the people who matter the most in my life, as opposed to people I deal with at work and life in general? That's one of the reasons I wrote this book. I have to remind myself of some basic nice principles—not so much at work, but in dealing with the people I love. I know I'm not the only one.

But I have had to train myself not to react the way I want to react when I am frustrated. I now count from one to ten before saying anything. I can have a snide comment (or clever remark in my book) ready to fire off, but counting off usually cools me down and I know it's not worth the argument or winning that round.

One evening, I was on the phone with my boyfriend. It was late and, frankly, I was exhausted. It had been a long day and I was not in the mood for chit chat. I should have just nicely ended the phone conversation saying goodnight and we would speak in the morning, yet I found myself discussing a contract for a new role I had just signed and leave entitlements.

It wasn't long until I started an argument about what type of holiday we should take and when we should take it. I also accused him of not listening to me and being selfish: two rather strong accusations to make within a two-minute conversation.

Surprisingly, my boyfriend got off the phone pretty quickly. He wasn't rude back to me and he didn't bite back; he just said goodnight. I went straight to sleep.

The next morning, I woke up feeling fresh and rather guilty. When you act from a place of anger (which I did), guilt is usually the accompanying emotion. I was rude and unreasonable to the person closest to me because I was tired. I would never react to my friends that way. I argued with myself all the way to work until I knew I couldn't start my day without apologising—it was the right thing to do. I just didn't want to do it.

I finally called my boyfriend—who thought something was wrong, as I never call him at work—and apologised (albeit gritting my teeth while doing so). He was very surprised and happy to hear my apology and readily accepted it after laughing at me.

The thing is, we can often talk ourselves out of apologising and make excuses for our behaviour. You can excuse the behaviour away all you want, but you still have to go home to that person every day. They say charity starts at home.

Dr Phil McGraw says it best in my opinion; whenever a couple is in the middle of an issue, he asks: *"Do you want to be right or do you want to be happy?"* Choose your battles wisely, especially on the home front.

When you are mistreated by your spouse, Pastor Jimmy Evans writes that you have a few options: responding to your spouse in a loving manner, receiving the hurt and hiding our feelings (i.e. passive aggressive behaviour), rejecting your spouse, (i.e., a form of revenge) or redeeming your spouse through righteous proactive behaviour—and, in doing so, demonstrating your love to that person.

How are you going to respond to your partner when there is hurt or unkindness sent your way? This answer will determine the destiny of your marriage or partnership.

There's no point making everyone happy at work if you can't keep the peace in your own home.

I hate being wrong. But I hate it more when people refuse to admit they are wrong—don't be that person. Eat the pie.

Be friendly—Focus on Connection

"Success can make you go one of two ways.
It can make you a prima donna—or it can smooth the edges,
take away the insecurities, let the nice things come out."
—Barbara Walters

When you're from a small town, people are genuinely interested in you. Where you came from, where you went to school—they really want to know. There is a motivation here: they usually want to know your last name, but don't want to come out and ask for it.

In the south, your family name is the most important asset you have. When we spoke about a friend or introduced them to our parents, one of the first questions asked is *"Who are your parents?"* Maybe your parents did the same, but I didn't notice this trend until years later. When you move to a big city, people are more interested in what you do for a living or where you live. But, your name—your family, and where you came from—inevitably says a lot about you.

They say the only thing money can't buy is your health or your reputation. It's up to you to manage those as best you can.

One day, my mother pulled into at a petrol store to fill up her tank. She got to talking to the attendant inside the shop. He asked her who her father was and, after hearing my grandfather's name, said that there would be no charge.

The only explanation he gave? *"If you're Kenneth's daughter, it's free."*

My grandfather was a good man. He wasn't rich, but he was just 'one of those people' that would help you out on the road if you were stranded. He wasn't a bragger, just a doer.

You have to wonder what he did for that man that affected him so much that, years later, just having his name gave my mother a wonderful gift that day—and it wasn't just a free tank of gas, but pride in her family name. Whatever it was, my grandfather's kind act was remembered and repaid years down the track.

Karma is a funny thing. Sometimes we don't actually see the 'fruit' of that tree blossom, but it does blossom—it might not just happen in front of you.

My sisters and I took a trip back to our hometown several years ago. Our father died when I was twelve years old and we wanted to come back and reconnect with family and friends. We had been out of the country for about 5 years.

Now, the thing you have to understand about my dad is that he was quiet. A good man, but a quiet one. As opposed to my mother who is (ahem)... the opposite. A great communicator, we would say! A lot of people knew our mama.

We borrowed a very nice car from our aunt for this trip. It was luxurious and we were nervous about keeping it in pristine condition. One day, we were driving and noticed a red light on the dashboard that would not stop flashing. We checked everything we could, but the light was still on and we had no way of turning it off. We decided to have it looked at straight away and pulled into a nearby mechanic. We were nervous. What was the problem? How much would it cost? We sat in the waiting room while the mechanic went to have a look.

The lady at reception noticed us and just started asking questions: *"Are you sisters?"* Yes. *"Wow, you look alike."* Thanks. We get that a lot. *"Are you from around here?"*

We really weren't in the mood. We wanted to know what was wrong with the car so that we could just get on with our trip and find a way to pay for it, but of course we smiled and were polite.

Then she asked *"Who are your parents?"* We told her. She stopped. *"Are you Bill's daughters? I don't know your mom, but I certainly knew Bill. We used to work together."*

You could have seen flies come out of our mouths.

She proceeded to tell us how they would have breaks together and her memories of him. She got to see a side of our dad we never did. She said he spoke about us girls and how proud he was of his family.

It was one of the most incredible gifts I have ever been given—her memories of someone we loved dearly.

I tell this story because it amazed me that she could have easily gone about her day and not even spoken to us. We would have gone about our day never even knowing we had crossed paths with someone who knew our father.

You have no idea what memories you have of someone, what information or encouragement you can impart on someone today. It just starts with: *"Hi, where are you from?"*

By the way, the car was fine. Someone (I'm pretty sure it wasn't me) had forgotten to screw the cap on the gas lid. The visit to the mechanic cost nothing, but we gained a friend and a story for a lifetime.

You are Uber nice

Did you know that Uber drivers give YOU a rating as a customer? I had no idea when I first started using the service that they were, in fact, also rating me. I was in the car with my husband—a very nice guy, who is usually quite reserved when we're out in public.

I couldn't help but notice on this one trip we took to the airport that he was very chatty to our Uber driver. When we were entering the airport, I saw him checking his app. That's when I found out not only can you rate the driver, but the driver also rates you.

Since then, we've been competing to see who can get the highest rating (I wish I could say it's me, but he's been the long-standing champion for a while now).

The point is, if you were rated every day on the quality of your courtesy—the way you treat people, family members, strangers on the street, your co-workers or the bus driver— what do you think your rating would be?

If people had to rate you every day on your nice rating, what would it be? This isn't about faking it; real courtesy comes from an attitude of serving your fellow man, but you have to start with deliberate action that doesn't always feel natural or normal at first.

This is where you consciously look for people to let ahead of you in line, or look to pay for a meal for a homeless person. You can train yourself to be a nicer person by starting to do nice things—the desire to replicate these acts of service will follow.

If you speak kind words and start doing kind things on a regular basis, your perspective will change. If you act it, you will feel it. Joy doesn't come to lazy people.

It's a life hack—a way of training yourself to be happy and kind.

Leo Witrich, the co-founder of Buffer, wrote a blog about the science of smiling: research shows that even the act of smiling helps others and your own cortisol levels go down. Faking a smile can cause real feelings of joy—even more than chocolate! Smiling reinforces our brain's reward mechanisms more than chocolate can and can actually change the brain's chemistry.

By even just performing the act of smiling more, you are training yourself to be more joyful.

CHAPTER

9

Excuse me, will you be my Oprah?

"A mentor is someone who allows you to see the hope inside yourself. A mentor is someone who allows you to see the higher part of yourself when sometimes it becomes hidden to your own view."
—Oprah Winfrey

I grew up watching Oprah. I remember racing home from school so I could catch her show on CBS, and would watch with fascination as she interviewed people from all walks of life. I loved how she just seemed like an everyday woman who was talking about real things. I said to my Dad, *"I want to be just like Oprah when I grow up."*

He told me I should write her a letter, which I did. And, while I am still anxiously awaiting Ms Winfrey's response, she has had an impact on me and how I would show up in my professional life, as well as millions of others across the world.

She has, in effect, been my mentor: a woman in media, a woman who talks about faith and spirituality, a woman who seeks to find the truth and connect people by using her platforms for storytelling.

You hear it all the time—get a mentor. I am a firm believer in finding people who can role model who you want to be, the job you want to have, the body you'd like to create, the marriage you'd like to be in.

A coach can help give you a game plan that is personal to you. A mentor can guide you over time, in a particular field that is relevant to you. I have had coaches on and off throughout the years, but I always have a mentor I can go to for sage advice.

There are two types of mentors: 'in your life' mentors and 'media mentors'. Both are important.

'In your life mentors'

In your life mentors include people who know you, encourage you, hire you or have a hand in getting you that job. They can explain office politics or how things 'really work' in the office. They are the people you call when that woman in accounting is being a nightmare, or you have a big project you'd like to pitch and don't know how to approach it. They understand the industry you are in (or would like to be in) and are further ahead then you.

These are your people. They are on the sidelines, in the background, coaching you from afar and letting you run with it. Your Yoda who will give you sage advice, your Oprah who will say, *"Go for it girl!"* when you need that real-life encouragement.

When you find these people, don't let them go.

When they give you advice, use it.

When they say, *"If I can help let me know,"* believe them. Get in touch when you need something. And stay in touch.

People love to help, but they're also busy. One of the most awkward things you can ask someone is if they will be your mentor. It feels like a huge responsibility, and smart, busy people would likely graciously decline such a request.

In my experience, a better approach is this: *"Can I buy you a coffee? I'd love to pick your brain about this job opportunity I have coming up."* Or, *"Do you have 10 minutes this week? I would love to know a bit more about your role and how you got there."* Be clear about what you are after and respect their time.

Take their advice. It's a slap in the face when someone recommends you reach out to Joe from marketing or to read that latest business book and you don't do it. It shows you don't value their advice or expertise.

When I was working as a publicist, I really enjoying hearing the producers talk about how they put the show together. I found myself being pulled to the production side of things, which felt awkward, but I wanted to explore it more.

I asked one of the producers out for a coffee, to get a sense of what they did and how they did it. It was only a fifteen minute chat, but I found out so much information—enough to make me know that I was interested in exploring this further.

I ended up asking the Executive Producer if I could work on their show for a while and worked in production for eight weeks with the team. I spoke to my manager and they kindly allowed me the time to work with the team and backfilled my publicity role.

It would have been hard for them to say no; they knew that the more I understood about the work they did, the better publicist I would be. I loved that experience and it certainly helped me speak with more credibility to producers in future roles.

Allow yourself to be curious. If you are interested in a role, ask about it—don't die wondering. This is the hustle part—the part where you have a really awkward five-minute conversation that could potentially change your career.

If you don't ask, you don't get. And, sometimes, a friendly chat with someone in the arena you want to be in is all you need to get started.

Some mentors are people who you watch from afar in the office and you think *"They know what they're doing."* They serve as an example of how you'd like to show you at work. I used to just watch their interactions, when they spoke up, when they were silent. I studied them as much as I could in a very un-stalkerlike fashion.

What I learned from 'in my life mentors':

- *How to write a professional yet personal email (just by reading their emails)*
- *How to have a polite but firm conversation (just by listening to their phone manners)*
- *When to draw the line at certain projects and expectations (just by being in meetings)*
- *When to move on from a role (by seeing when they decided to move on or go for the next stage)*

Notice here: I learned from these people by observing their behaviours in the workplace. Others I learned from by having coffee with them when I had specific questions about a role I was interested in or issues I was having at work, or when I needed a sounding board to help me find out what the next level was.

Here are some ways to keep **'In my life'** mentors in your corner:

- *Remember their birthday*
- *Send a Christmas card or a thank you card once a year*
- *If you see an article that reminds you of them, send it over*

- *Never stop saying thank you or reaching out, even when you have moved on*
- *When leaving a role or career, personally let them know or update them*
- *Remember the names of people in their family*
- *Ask how you can help them. You may not feel you have anything to give right now, but you might be surprised at their response*

When people feel you value them, they will stay in your corner for years to come.

Media mentors

My other mentors... well, these people don't even know I exist. But I learn as much as they are willing to share.

Media mentors are pretty powerful and offer a way to get free advice and coaching. I love podcasts. I cannot get enough of hearing successful people talk about their journey, strategies, inspiration, and perspectives I may have never thought of before. I love reading books on success, watching interviews—anything that will help spark an idea, inspire me to take action or help me look at something differently.

Some of my favourite media mentors include (in no order): *TD Jakes, Oprah, Michelle Obama, Candace Cameron Bure, Lewis Howe, John Maxwell, Priscilla Shirer, Stephen Furtick, Gina Devee, Carrie Green, Ed Mylett, Tony Robbins, Donald Miller, Rachel Hollis, Phil McGraw, Marie Forleo, Lisa Bevere, Gary Vanderchuck, Freedom Church, Proverbs 31 ministries.*

I could go on. But the point is that I listen to a variety of people who have expertise or experience in a variety of areas. I don't go to one role model for everything. If I want to learn how to manage people, I go to someone with a management style I respect. If I want to improve my relationships, I go to someone who I believe has the type of relationship I want to be in.

Not one person will have everything you need—pick your person for their expertise in that one thing and let them be your Yoda for that issue.

Look at the results they have had. If you want what they have, find out what they did and do it. Pick your work Yoda, your marriage Yoda, your health Yoda. Let them show you how they created the success you admire—and copy it.

It sounds simple, but it's not easy. I've found that sometimes a person may be incredible at office politics but not so great at personal relationships. And that's ok. Don't let that put you off taking their advice in the areas they excel at.

Prayer, wisdom and faith

I love the chapter of Proverbs in the Bible. It's like life hacks of wisdom you can apply in every area of life. I can spout out a lot of life experience here, but the truth is my intuition and trust in God has been and continues to be foundational to everything I do.

Prayer is a powerful thing. I pray every day to have the wisdom of Solomon and the favour of David.

Because sometimes life is grey. Wisdom is not.

In Proverbs 13.20, it says "*Whoever walks with the wise becomes wise, but the companion of fools will suffer harm.*"

Make sure the person you're getting advice from deserves your attention. If they've not yet achieved what you want to have in your life or career, I would smile graciously and move on to find the person who can actually give you wisdom you need.

If you want to star in the NBA, find out how much Michael Jordan trained each day and copy it. If you want to get a book published, look at how many publishers JK Rowling approached before getting *Harry*

Potter onto bookshelves. If you want to work for the United Nations as the Director of Communications, find out who has (or has had) that role. Research them and find out their steps.

Become obsessive in studying the person you want to become. Find out what they did, what daily habits they had, and do it for yourself.

Take note: even the experts can only take you so far. Unless you are talking to God or reading the Bible, everyone and everything else can only offer so much. Don't expect perfection from your role models. I love Oprah, but she's human just like you and me. I admire her success and give grace for areas I might not like or agree with.

Because I hope people will do the same for me when I need it.

Only God is perfect. The rest of us are a work in progress. But He will strategically place people in our path who will help us get to where we need to be. Be open and intentional about discovering who that person can be for you right now.

Exercise: Make a list of five people in your life (or who you know of) who you'd love to be in your corner around your career. Pray on it. In the next 48 hours, reach out to them personally and invite them for coffee or ask for a phone chat. Be specific in what exactly you desire from that conversation. Keep it simple. Tell them why you are thinking of them, ask for their time and press send.

CHAPTER

10

Mind your manners (and watch your mouth)

"Forget the mistake. Remember the lesson."
—Lisa Messenger

If you treat everyone the same—from the cleaner to the CEO—you never have to worry about how you treated someone or who you spoke to.

I was in the elevator with a colleague and we were talking about our plans for an upcoming long weekend. I happened to be working. She queried why and I gave a rather snide remark about how the producers *"never get holidays,"* so I shouldn't expect to either.

Little to my knowledge, I had one of the producers on that very elevator, who then made his presence known. He made it clear that he didn't appreciate my complaining; he'd been working for 18 days straight and said that I should consider myself lucky.

Nice guy *cough.*

However, I should have known better.

What were the chances of being in the same elevator as the person I was talking about? Very little. But it happened, and I could have easily avoided that #awkward moment by considering my words more carefully.

I was told later that this person was not very liked within the team, but it didn't make me feel any better. I knew I had succumbed to just saying what I felt like and hadn't considered the impact of my words. I believe we have all been in a similar experience, which could have been entirely prevented if I had thought before I talked.

Even in a confrontational discussion, which we all have to have from time to time (especially in the workplace), Dale Carnegie has awesome advice for placating a difficult conversation: **You will never get in trouble by admitting you may be wrong about something.**

In his famous book, *How to Win Friends and Influence People*, he interviews a number of successful people, noting that their accomplishments could usually be attributed to their diplomacy skills: *"I am convinced that nothing good is accomplished and a lot of damage can be done if you tell out a person straight that he or she is wrong. You only succeed in stripping that person of self-dignity and making yourself an unwelcome part of any discussion."*

When the most obvious course of action seems to be to point out the facts, it is actually better in the long term to take five minutes and sit in the position of someone who could be wrong about an issue. We could all do with being a little quieter.

Before you speak, ask yourself: how is what you are saying affecting someone else? Are you encouraging or thanking someone? Or are you complaining and gossiping? Think about every sentence in your head that is begging to come out—what is the motivation?

Take charge of your words and know that, if you say them, you must own them—you never know who could be standing right behind you in an elevator.

If you can't be complimentary, you can at least be quiet (something I have learned the hard way, time and time again!).

CHAPTER

11

Aren't you a sight for sore eyes? (Never underestimate welcoming a person)

"What separates privilege from entitlement is gratitude."
—Brene Brown

One of my first cousins got in touch with my mom about a friend of theirs. She had met this man online and was travelling to Sydney to see him. They were worried about her safety and being a single woman on her own. As I was living in Sydney at the time, they asked if she could have my mobile number in case something went wrong.

I said sure, and didn't think much of it after that.

A few weeks later, I got a call from a lady named Dawn. The voice-mail was concerning: she said she needed help and a place to stay. We organised to meet at a local train station near my house. I left work, met

Dawn and took her to my apartment. I told her she was welcome to stay for the rest of her trip.

Returning to work, I told my colleagues what had happened (and why I had to leave so fast). They seemed shocked.

"Do you know her?" they asked.

I said no, but my cousins do.

"What if she's crazy, or steals from you?"

All I knew was how I was raised. When someone is in need—and you can—you help. I also knew she was from the south and my family vouched for her. Where I come from, when family vouches for a person, you treat them like a member of your own family. That's just the way it works.

Fortunately, Dawn wasn't crazy and she wasn't a thief (not that I had much to steal!). She was lovely, fun, smart, and she spent the next two weeks at my apartment. I made a friend for life and I know I always have a place to stay whenever I go to Florida. That golden rule doesn't say "*do unto others if you have checked out their criminal background and ensured they aren't insane*"—it says do unto others as you would have them do unto you.

Having someone (even a complete stranger) welcome you into your home can be one of the greatest gifts you can give to a person—whether it be a colleague, a new neighbour, or someone you hear is having a rough time. Please know I'm not advocating for inviting complete strangers into your home; if you don't feel comfortable or safe, don't do it. It's about seeing a need, and being open to meeting it.

My mother made good friends with her mailwoman and often invited her in for coffee. Neighbours thought that was strange and intrusive having someone in your home regularly, but think about it: everyone is in need of the same thing—to be acknowledged or cared for.

I don't care what country you are from, it's a universal theme.

That's the southern way—everybody is welcome—and it's a gift that keeps on giving.

Be genuinely happy to see and meet someone

You can tell a lot about a person by how they treat the janitor. Do they ignore them? Say thank you when they pass them in the hallway or acknowledge them? What about the new intern?

In my early media days, I did work experience in the news room of a local television station. It was a small team and I would usually spend a day with each of the journalists to see how they put together a news package that would wind up on the air that evening. It was exciting stuff for a newbie. As most enthusiastic interns did, I went up to the main news presenter at the time and introduced myself. To say that the news-reader was dismissive of me is an understatement. I was almost shocked at how rude she was and thought maybe I caught her on a bad day. Turns out I hadn't. She was known for that type of behaviour.

Ironically, a year later, I was doing intern work for the local newspaper and was sent to cover an event she was an ambassador for. She didn't recognise me, of course, and she was sweet as pie to me; as I would be writing up her quotes for the paper, she had a lot of time (and pleasantries) for me.

It was a stark difference from the introduction we had a year before. I was polite, of course, but it taught me the importance of spending just one minute with someone when you meet them—you never know what they may end up writing about you one day.

In contrast, one of the columnists for the paper I was interning for was a popular icon—everyone knew him. I loved reading his column and had hoped to meet him. Turns out I did—he came up to me and was looking for someone.

He was so polite. He introduced himself straight away and asked me a question, and that was it. He made such a strong impression on me, though we barely spoke for a minute. He was just ... nice. And I'll always remember that.

Dr Phil McGraw writes in his book *Life Code* that he doesn't care how people treat him; he knows people are usually on their best behaviour to his face. What he wants to know is how someone treated his driver, producer, or the people at the hotel.

That is the measure of someone: how they treat those who can do nothing for them.

CHAPTER
12

Don't have a hissy fit when things don't go your way

*"You will never regret being kind. And you can
trust even if you don't see its side effects, your actions
are rippling outward to make a difference."*
—*Candace Cameron Bure*

Working in television can be fun.

Going to see live recordings of shows, actors doing interviews, hanging out in the green room watching interesting people talk about their careers—it is fascinating. It is also enlightening; you get to see the 'dark side' of people in the limelight. Some people are used to having others at their beckoned call.

I have seen respectable adults have literal tantrums because they can't find their tie or a script has gone astray, or they have hurt themselves and need an army of people around to coo them into health.

There is a lot of power in the television industry. Executives and actors or presenters hold it—the rest of us work around it, and are at the mercy of their attitude.

As I said before, television is a tense environment. You're only as good as your last show, so stakes are high. But even people who 'made it,' who have no dues to pay, still have the power to make your day a living nightmare.

I'm not here to name and shame… just to share some stories.

I was working on a photo shoot with about fifteen people who worked across the media, television, and film. It was an entertaining day, and just a fun environment to be around. A particular journalist was very popular at our television network. I had never worked with her, but heard stories. I always reserve judgement until I meet someone, so I had no ill-conceived preconceptions of her. She was in a jolly mood, flirting with younger men, but said she had a bruise on her leg and needed help replacing a bandage. I was not her assistant. I did not work with this lady; in fact I had never met her before.

She asked me to get her some tape. I did as requested. She then asked me to put the tape on the bandage on her leg. I thought it was stretching the friendship, but I like being helpful. I gently placed the tape on her leg. She screamed. Literally.

"You're HURTING me!!!!"

I stopped, completely shocked. I had barely touched this woman, did not know her, and she was screaming in my face, in front of dozens of people.

"I'll do it myself!" she screamed, and snatched the tape from me. I stood up and left the room.

I still had to deal with her that day, and was as professional as possible. No one said anything about that incident, but her colours shined bright that day. I was annoyed but, more than that, embarrassed for her. No thank you—she never even asked my name. Then she went about flirting with her young men and smiling at the people that 'mattered' (read: other television presenters). Everyone else (myself included) were just there for her to acknowledge when she was in need of something.

I have been yelled at many times in television. You get used to it. It's unnatural, really; outside of a TV studio, if someone had spoken to me that way, her behaviour would have been unacceptable.

Another presenter yelled at me in front of the crew because I asked for him to approve copy so we could meet a deadline. He used some unsavoury language and told me to get out. I did. He later emailed me an apology, which I was grateful for, but it wasn't the last time he did it. A TV host I worked with was polite to me, but treated his wardrobe mistress appallingly. He would snap his fingers at her, asking for his jacket. I will always remember that: too smart to be rude to the publicist, but too careless to show basic courtesy to one of the crew members. It didn't leave me with the nicest impression (and I really wanted to like this guy).

I have also worked with incredibly kind and talented people who somehow knew how to control their emotions and not take it out on people around them. It didn't mean they weren't frustrated when things weren't going to schedule, but they didn't blame people in the process. They just wanted to get the job done and were nice enough along the way. They were a gift to be around, and I would happily work longer and harder for them just because they make life a lot more pleasant.

In television, as in life, you have to improvise. Things never go according to script, but how you react to those curbs really shows the type of person you are. When things aren't going your way, it is much easier to 'let someone have it', then it is to take a breath, get over it, and move on.

It is not anyone else's business if you are having a bad day. When you are NICE, you:

> **N**ever let your mood/day affect your attitude
> **I**nstigate the apology or ice breaker
> **C**are for others first
> **E**veryone matters

CHAPTER

13

You get more flies with honey than vinegar

"The most courageous act is still to think for yourself. Aloud."
—Coco Chanel

I worked for one manager who was considered by many to be a bully. She certainly had a particular way of getting what she wanted in the workplace. She believed in aggressively winning, getting the job done, and putting yourself first. I learned a lot from this manager. I learned in being confident, knowing my skill set, and my professional value in a team, and for that I was grateful.

I also learned that people will respond to aggression; usually, they will forfeit for the sake of peace. But there is always a cost.

As soon as this boss left our team, a mood lifted. We worked as a team again. Problems could be solved by talking not yelling. She wasn't missed when she left the building.

On the contrary, I had another manager who, when I made a mistake (and I was always the first to admit it), we would talk through the problem and find the solution—that was it. There was no berating. It was a mistake that could be dealt with.

Her 'nice' attitude meant I would say yes to whatever request she would ask of me, because I *wanted* to help and I knew any mistakes made would not leave me in fear of losing my job. She had a sweet disposition and would get things accomplished at work through diplomacy and communication.

She was also a pleasant person to deal with. Did I enjoy coming into work after that? Absolutely. Would I ever work for the previous boss again? Not if I had a choice.

I would rather work with a 'nice person' who can learn the ropes than someone who uses bullying and not-nice principles to work.

There is actually a 'Bring Your Manners To Work' Day. Yep. It's a thing, like National Children's Day—which I'm pretty sure did not exist when I was a kid, because apparently little ones don't get enough attention nowadays *cough.*

I digress… but seriously. This unique day of awareness was created by The Protocol School of Washington to remind people of the importance of treating people with courtesy and respect in the workplace.

Do we really need a national day of awareness to tell us to be polite to each other? Apparently so. Lund University in Sweden surveyed nearly 6,000 people and their studies showed that being subjected to rudeness is a major reason for dissatisfaction at work—and, if not addressed, can be contagious to those around you.

Manners are becoming as rare as old vinyl players—the real old ones that you find in Salvos that weigh about the size of a piano, not the £30 one you can get at Urban Outfitters (no judgement here, I own one too). They are rare to find, totally awesome and everyone loves to be around them.

I know I would much rather work with someone less experienced that's polite and nice to be around than someone at the top of their game who doesn't engage in basic manners.

Some days, I'm really not in the mood to act like Pollyanna—particularly when I'm having a crappy time (or when a Netflix binge got out of control the night before)—but, as my mother always said, *"If you can't be nice, at least be quiet."* When just the sound of an office phone makes me want to throw my stapler at someone, this piece of advice has always been a life saver.

I'm a fan of manners. Even though there will always be people at work who don't seem to hold them in the same regard, the least I can do is treat them the way I want to be treated, so says the Golden rule. It's an international remedy that works in almost every situation.

My family and I regularly stayed at a small beach resort for an annual vacation. My mother loved this one particular house because it was in such close proximity to the beach, so she ensured that she called six months in advance of our trip to book it for our vacation.

She was assured that it was reserved. However, when we eventually arrived—the entire family in tow—for our vacay, we had a receptionist who was less than exemplary in her customer service skills. We were told we did not have the house we had reserved; it wasn't possible for them to reserve 'particular' houses, so my mother must had been mistaken.

Aside from the bad news she was giving, her manner was haughty and rude.

I was ready to give her a piece of my mind; my mother went the other, wiser way. She finally found out the owners had decided to stay in the house—thus the change of plans. As a result of the way we were treated by this one person, our family has decided not to re-book at this resort again. Customers vote with their feet.

The truth was the problem could have been so easily alleviated by a phone call and apologies; there could have been some good graces exchanged. Unfortunately, the way this particular receptionist handled the issue made us feel disrespected, and you don't usually freely give money to people who make you feel that way.

Sometimes a girl's just gotta have her say: Dealing with a bully as a classy gal

I'm not naive. There are times when, particularly at work, a confronting conversation or an awkward talk needs to take place. You have been as kind as humanly possible, and gone the extra mile, politely addressed issues and yet, one of two things have happened: you continue to get undermined or walked over by a colleague or a manager, or things have escalated.

I have always found it easier to confront people in my personal life more than at work. I choose my battles wisely, so this has only happened about three times in my career. If you feel things have continued to such a point that they will be untenable if you continue, then a confrontation is essential.

The most challenging confrontation I had to face was one with my line manager. I managed a small team and felt regularly undermined by her decisions; she had a habit of starting disagreements in front of the team. I felt targeted on a daily basis. Not only was it undermining my authority as a manager, I started dreading work and remained in a constant state of anxiety, as my manager's requirements would change from one hour to the next.

I don't believe her manner was intentional (but incredibly unprofessional), but no matter how many times I tried to address the issue, there was no difference in her behaviour. I had no idea what the outcome of a confrontation would be. I just knew I could not continue as things were—for my own sanity, and for the team I was working with.

I didn't do this quickly or easily but, once I did, it completely changed our working relationship; frankly, my manager respected me for standing up to her. I didn't just let her have it one day, as much as I desperately wanted to. I prepared an action plan and delivered it in the politest way I knew how.

Here's my handy action plan for how to deal with a genuine bully when you have to keep working with them:

Step 1: Seek advice
I sought the assistance of an in-house mentor so I could have an objective perspective. You can also privately approach someone in HR.

Step 2: Book a day and time
Find a time and place that suits you. I ensured we went outside the office to neutral territory (we went to a nearby coffee shop).

Step 3: Keep emotion out
There were many days I went to the bathroom to cry because of the pressure I felt. These are not the right days to confront someone. I waited until I had a clear head and had prepared myself mentally for the conversation that would come.

Step 4: Be prepared
I made a list of issues and concerns, followed by suggested solutions. Solutions are crucial; otherwise, it will just be a list of things you are whining about—no one wants to hear that.

Your solutions should offer a positive/amicable way of moving forward and working together. One of my issues was the way the manager spoke to a junior member of our team. She was incredibly cruel to him at times, and pretty much everyone observed this behaviour.

My manager could not discern what was joking and what perceived as unkind commentary, so I offered this solution: we agreed on a code word. This was her signal that things were getting out of hand. She loved it because she genuinely didn't have a filter for what was appropriate in work conversation. This document needs to demonstrate the issues you are facing that impact the team's performance or your individual person. Pick your issues wisely. If you have more than five to discuss, then the other person may see this as a personal attack and will be less responsive.

Step 5: Start off nicely

Thank the person for taking the time to meet, and discuss anything else you can think of that would start the conversation lightly, and not put the person on defence. If you can think of something to compliment them on (their strengths at work), then this would be a good time to bring them up.

Step 6: Remain confident

It is easier to think of reasons NOT to have this meeting, but to remain confident in your position and gain respect in the workplace, this has to occur. Confronting does not mean accusing. You can't argue with how someone feels, so start with phrases such as: *"When you told the team to only focus on social media and I had an afternoon of meetings with them, which we had already agreed to, I felt undermined."*

Step 7: Finish nicely

It is likely this conversation will include a great deal of feedback on both ends. Ensure you get through all the points you have outlined and, once finished, say thank you and that you are open to any feedback.

Step 8: Follow up

After the meeting, follow up with an email that outlines the discussion you had. It could be short and sweet, just reiterating the conversation you had and that you look forward to working better together, or you could email the list you discussed. The email chain shows you are serious about these issues and gives you a paper trail in case you need it down the road.

I can't guarantee that the person on the receiving end will always react well, but this formula ensures you protect yourself professionally and ethically.

When you have a difficult person in your life or work, a nice person still assumes the best of people. However, if a person has regularly proved that they are not as respectful as you, boundaries must be created. You are the only one who can do that—in the nicest possible way, of course.

You will feel more in control and it's likely your relationship with this person will improve, or at least diffuse. If things don't improve, I would look at my next professional step. You cannot continue to work when you are feeling anxious and undermined. Take your body's cue and get yourself into a different environment.

People respect those with clear boundaries, and it's your job to make sure these boundaries are communicated. Put your big girl pants on and have the conversation.

Sticks and stones may break my bones, but your words will hurt me more

"Don't waste your energy trying to change opinions...
Do your thing and don't care if they like it."
—Tina Fey

There is nothing more effective and bewildering than being nice to those who have been hurtful to you in the past. Everyone has a conscience. It is so easy to dismiss people when they are rude to us, but just imagine someone who you were unfairly rude to—perhaps a co-worker or a person at a coffee shop. If they continue to show you nothing but kindness, how can that not make you question yourself and make you feel... well, really crappy?

The take home message is: the way people treat you is a statement of who they are as a human being. It is not a statement about you.

Read this again: **it's not about you.**

As you get older, you'll understand more and more that life's not about what you look like or what you own—it's all about the person you've become. Niceness makes you a better person. Get in the habit of developing it.

You can't change how people treat you or what they say about you. All you can do is change how you react to it. Kindness is for your own health. Every negative thought you have, your body cells react negatively. As we have discussed before, being kind can literally change the wiring in your brain and give you a happy high.

But what if you only choose to think about the times that people did you wrong? What about when a co-worker gossiped about you, you were treated poorly in a relationship, a relative made offensive comments and never supported your dream? Surely you shouldn't just let that go? Yes. You should. And you can. Not only is it possible, but if you want to live a free, happy, and healthy life, then kindness (and forgiveness) is the only option.

It's simple, but it's not easy. But if you don't let grace lead in these moments, you'll spend so much of your energy holding onto issues that were never yours to begin with.

No one said it was easy, but the personal freedom and benefits you will get from taking out your emotional trash can actually transform your life. Words do hurt. We know this. But don't let them keep hurting you even after they are spoken.

If you truly think something was just 'too bad' for you to let go, consider these real stories of kindness that may put things into perspective for you:

- Julio Diaz offered his coat to the man who stole his wallet. The two ended up having dinner and a life-changing conversation together.

- Beautician Katie Cutler raised over £320,000 for a disabled man who was violently mugged outside his house in Gateshead, England.

- After a long shift at the fire department, Matt Swatzell fell asleep while driving and crashed into another vehicle, taking the life of pregnant mother June Fitzgerald and injuring her 19-month-old daughter. According to <u>Today</u>, Fitzgerald's husband, a full-time pastor, asked for the man's diminished sentence and began meeting with Swatzell for coffee and conversation. Many years later, the two men remain close.

- Domestic violence survivor Pascale Kavanagh said that she never thought she would reconnect with her mother—her abuser—during her adult life. However, in 2010, her mother suffered several strokes that left her unable to communicate or take care of herself. With no one else to help, Kavanagh began to sit by her mother's bedside and read to her. Through this, Kavanagh says the hate she had for her mother dissipated into forgiveness and love.

Cue the waterworks...

There are numerous stories of how people have forgiven what most of us would see as the unforgivable, and looked past their own trouble to help those who are doing it tough. I am not saying this to undermine or devalue any pain in your own life; I say this to put your pain in perspective. And really ask what the payoff is for holding onto stuff from the past, because I can guarantee you it's robbing you from something in your future.

We've all been hurt. Some more than others. But we all face a choice on what to do with that pain. The people in your life are there for a reason and a purpose. Don't let them own you and limit what you could give to this world.

CHAPTER
15

An email is nice; a card is nicer (Going the extra mile)

"Always be a first-rate version of yourself instead of a second-rate version of somebody else"
—Judy Garland

I remember when I went for my first interview in television. It was my first publicist role and, while I had been working in the media industry for the last two years, I wasn't exactly a perfect fit.

I was so nervous. I remember the anxiety I felt walking into the interview. I wish I could say that the butterflies left, and I hit a home run, but that was not the case. It was one of the worst interviews I've ever had. I was tongue-tied, could feel my cheeks getting red, couldn't answer certain questions that should have been easy... it was downright embarrassing. I walked out and cried on the way home.

My mother had taught me two things growing up: do everything you can in a situation and then let it go and give it to God. I went home and wrote a thank you letter to the interviewers, posted it that day, said a quick prayer, then drowned my sorrows in chocolate. Handwritten notes are a rarity nowadays and little did I know how that one gesture would prove fateful to my next job.

One week later, I got a job offer. I was in shock, but didn't ask questions; I just quickly agreed and signed the contract so they wouldn't change their mind! After the first week, I dared to ask my boss why she hired me. I knew how poor my interview was. She said it was between myself and another girl; while the girl was more 'polished'— meaning here that she could string a sentence together—she didn't have the same enthusiasm I did. And it was the thank you card sealed the deal.

I went the extra mile to ensure that this person knew I wanted the job and I stood out with just a simple gesture and a nice attitude along with it.

Hack: Keep a stack of thank you cards in your desk and some stamps in your wallet. It's so much easier to quickly write a personal note when you don't need to go out and buy one!

Blimey—that was an easy email to write

While I was living in London, my flatmates and I had to get a new television. It turned into what I call now the TV saga. We had a new television delivered to us; within a week, it stopped working. I bought another television and was excited to get the thing working, but it turned out we were short four screws to actually connect the television to the stand. Not life-changing, but annoying nonetheless. When I went back to the store, I chatted with one of the employees about my dilemma.

This was in December, about two weeks before Christmas. It was a Saturday evening and the store was busy—I wasn't bringing in a sale and, frankly, he could have sent me on my way. But he didn't. He helped me.

He called the head office on my behalf and negotiated. This process took about twenty minutes and, while he was on the phone, he was helping other customers. My outcome was positive—I went back to the store the next day to pick up the screws, which had been specially delivered on my behalf.

It may sound simple, but these accessories were not available anywhere else and were sold separately. I told the guy who helped me how thankful I was, but I really felt he had gone the extra mile for me. The next day, I wrote an email to the head office, addressing it to the manager of the store, and didn't think much of it. I was just hoping he would get some kind of acknowledgement from his boss.

A few weeks later, I was back in the store again—this time as a regular, non-complaining customer. I happened to be served by this guy again. He called me the 'TV lady' and I just smiled.

"I saw the email you sent my boss," he said. *"That has never happened to me. Thank you so much."* His boss had sent the email to his team and had acknowledged his efforts. He then turned to his co-worker: *"Remember that customer who sent that email? This is her."*

A word about the British people. They are what I call 'understated' in terms of behaviour. I know if this same situation played out in Georgia, this employee would have hugged me and invited me to their church on Sunday. That is the southern way. But Londoners are not so overwhelming in their behaviour. That doesn't mean they don't show gratitude—they do—but it is a rare moment that they say more than a thank you and a nod for a gesture.

So, this guy's appreciation to me was a sweet moment.

That email literally took me 10 minutes to write and send, but here I had an employee who could tell me exactly what effect it had on him.

I know there are many times I have received great service, and I should have 'officially' passed on my gratitude but did not.

This experience reminded me of how important it is—not to you, but to others—to go that extra mile. You have no idea what battle that person is fighting and how much of an impact you can have on their day.

CHAPTER

16

The Grit, Grace and Hustle Challenge

"Don't be like the rest of them, darling"
—Grace Kelly

Aside from all this 'be nice to all' stuff I'm banging on about, there are practical ways you can improve your mindset, relationships, and everyday life. First, remind yourself on a daily basis of the person who you to show up as.

It is a well-known fact what you think you become—ensure the words you wake up to and go to sleep to are strong, positive messages. Surround yourself with nice quotes in your bedroom, bathroom mirror, on your keyboard at work. I often have a quote or scripture I love taped to the bathroom mirror so I can see it every day. And I repeat it out loud, several times. Consider this: your brain believes what you repeat. It believes your thoughts, your words, what you speak, and how you are spoken to.

Awesome energy attracts awesome people. Confidence attracts more confidence.

Depending on what I'm focusing on that season (becoming more giving, financial abundance, being more compassionate, more disciplined, etc.), I will choose a quote or create an affirmation that will encourage me in this particular area. Some examples of my favourites are below:

"I am a passionate, kind, fun, gorgeous and smart woman who is changing the world, in small ways and big ways every day. I am loved by God and I show His love to people every day. Me and God cannot fail." (My own affirmation for showing up as more loving and compassionate in the world).

For the next seven days, identify people in your life, work, community that you can reach out to (anonymously or in person) that cannot naturally or quickly repay you. This could be a stranger, work colleague, neighbour, church person, at the gym, waiter, flight attendant, or a person at a coffee shop.

For this challenge, I encourage you to try out seven acts of kindness for seven days:

1. *Pay it forward: pay for someone's coffee you don't know*
2. *Compliment a co-worker you don't know well*
3. *Pick up litter around your neighbourhood or take a neighbour's trash out*
4. *Send a thank you note to your local council person or favourite hangout*
5. *Write an email to someone from your old work to check in*
6. *Bake something for neighbours or your office*
7. *Cook a surprise dinner for someone*
8. *Offer to buy a meal for a homeless person (A lot of cafés have a suspended meal arrangement. Ask inside for details)*

These are just ideas, of course, but you get the point: set out every day to intentionally make someone's life easier or bless them in some way, with no expectation of return. Some days are harder than others to be selfless but, if you do this for seven days, I guarantee you there will be a shift. Maybe in your own home. Or you'll make a new connection. Maybe you'll get a job offer down the track that will change the course of your career, like I did.

Either way, you'll feel more empowered as you show up as the loving and selfless person you are. Confidence comes from doing, and from showing up as the person you want to be in life. The happier you make people, the happier you'll be in your own life.

While I was working at the BBC, there was a day I was on my way to work and saw a blind man. I was working in the city and there are many crossings outside the train station. I watched this man with fascination: he had a walking stick, but it was obvious he was completely blind and walking in a similar direction to me. I decided to walk closely to him and assist if I could (I admit, I felt sorry for him). A few times, I stopped him from walking into street signs and helped him to cross the road. We started talking and it turns out he also worked at the BBC. He had an amazing job as a journalist, was married and had a child. I went from feeling sorry for this man to being in awe of him—just from starting a conversation. As well as meeting a new colleague, it was also a lesson in judging a stranger's situation—you learn a lot more by just asking questions, being curious and offering to help.

Justine's story: "You should throw kindness around like confetti"

Some gestures can be literally life changing. When I was researching this book, I wanted to hear about the effect that kindness can have and get different perspectives. A dear friend of mine—Justine, who moved to Thailand—had an incredible experience she shared with me. Below is the story she sent me about how kindness has been a life saver for her.

"Life here is amazing, but it has been incredibly challenging to get set up. There is so much to be said for having a support network of your friends and family around you and being in a country that you can work in with ease. Embarking on this adventure alone has presented me with challenges that have shown me how incredible—and how much impact—the simplest gestures from the kindness of strangers can have. I believe you should throw kindness around like confetti; it is the 'richest' currency there is without being financially driven an iota. Here are some examples of how the smallest gestures have had a remarkable impact here on lifting my spirits:

Part of my adventure here has been training Muay Thai. The typical road to a foreigner preparing for a fight is to do a whole lot of private lessons, which come at a cost. I had been relying on selling my car to give me some extra stability while I set up my life here. It wasn't happening, and I couldn't see myself moving back to Australia. At this time, it happened to be low season at the Muay Thai gym I decided to call my fitness home. A trainer by the name of Moo started to take me under his wing and train me up. One day about a week into training together, while showing me a technique, he said, "I know you don't want to fight—you want to be fit and healthy... but if you change your technique to this..."

My response: "Well... actually I would like to?"

Things started to change from there. He took me under his wing and trained me one on one during the group classes, and quickly saw how dedicated my work ethic was. He started to really believe in me—that I could fulfil one of my dreams to compete in a pro Muay Thai fight—and invested more and more time and care every day into transforming me into a pro Muay Thai Fighter.

He did not have to do this—he wasn't getting paid extra—but he did it anyway, and he did it with joy. He believed in me during a time where

I was under immense financial pressure, mental pressure, and pressure to find a home, get a visa, and build a social network from scratch. In the beginning, he kept saying: "we have a year, every day you're a little bit better." Within two weeks I was improving out of sight; within four, I was officially part of the fight team. Within six, every trainer in the gym was in shock that I had improved out of sight and my first pro fight was scheduled. By the time it came to fight day at the eight week point, I had transformed into a Muay Thai Fighter. In two months, I had improved the amount normal for someone in one year.

NONE of this would have been possible without Kru Moo: his time, dedication and belief in me. What this belief did for my soul during such a challenging time, I have no words that could do it justice. Through fight training, I found my 'champion mindset' for life again. There were so many times I wanted to give up: injuries, fatigue, the mental challenges that go with learning new techniques and building the confidence of a fighter, to have 'No Fear.' I had stopped believing in myself fully after my Dad died fifteen years prior and life had been a struggle ever since. My heart had been broken wide open. I now felt unstoppable, that I could conquer any challenge thrown my way. THAT, grown from a simple act of kindness and incredible gesture of belief in someone, has been a catalyst for one of the most powerful gifts someone has every given me. Kru Moo has changed my life.

Along the way in the process, these gestures continued...

- *I was struggling with what I thought might be a broken toe. He drove twenty minutes out of his way to pick me up, take me to the massage place and talk to the masseuse in Thai to explain the specific treatment I needed. He said, "Don't worry, I take care of you."*
- *The Velcro on my hand wraps was no longer sticking and I was training twelve times a weeke tells me his friend gives him hand wraps all the time. He then rocked up to training; I had my crappy pair that day. He took them, thew them in the bin and came back*

with not one, but two new pairs! He said nothing, started wrapping my hands with one and threw the other in my bag

- Training was getting intense. I was covered in bruises and my feet were seizing into cramps. He said—again—"Don't worry, I take care of you," and came over with a hot water bottle and a special type of oil you need to travel ten hours to get as a gift for me, and treated my legs until the pain went away. He wouldn't accept money for any of this. "Don't worry, I gift to you."

- It was fight day and I hadn't bought a pair of shorts and top with the gym logo… I was waiting to transfer to the account I could access and had messed up the timing. I rocked up to the gym in my outfit, which I thought was fine. He asked me where my Sinbi clothes were, then said, "Don't worry, I take care of you," and bought the outfit for me at a discount. Being in the Sinbi gear made all the difference!

- After the fight, I could barely walk. My phone had been rained on a few days prior and, not being in Australia, I couldn't make an insurance claim. I could no longer use it, so no one could call me. The next day, I was lying in bed in agony, couldn't even get out of the house to get food. Moo rocked up at my doorstep with a bottle of 'Special drink,' a disgusting concoction of herbs that took all my will to consume, but had an amazing impact in reducing all the inflammation in my legs.

I never asked for any of these things and there were many more… Every gesture was an act of kindness without any expectation of something in return. The culmination of all these things—of someone simply 'taking care' of me when I was alone in a foreign country, facing many challenges—lifted my spirits beyond measure.

I went on to win my first Muay Thai fight against an opponent who was far more experienced, with six or seven fights to her name. She was by far the favourite. I won because I trained hard and had been taken care of, but *also because my heart was full. It had been topped up with so much belief and care that I was unstoppable.*

My life had been transformed before I even stepped into the ring because of the change internally. I could not be more grateful to Kru Moo for believing in me and the multitude of kind gestures that helped my rediscover and awaken my Champion Mindset. After fifteen long years of struggle in every way—financial, relationships, family, emotional—I now feel truly fearless and full of joy and happiness. This mental change is being transferred to my life with a rapidly growing network of great people, courageous new experiences, and two businesses I absolutely love growing and thriving. There is a childlike excitement that comes with the creation of the life you've imagined... knowing it IS all possible. I believe we can all achieve anything we set our minds on, let love lead, fail fast, and keep going despite the odds. Know in your heart: "You are a Champion."

This journey has been a beautiful reminder that even the smallest gesture that may be of no consequence to your own life can make a huge impact on another. It is a beautiful challenge, to wake up and think, "How can I make a difference to someone's life today?" LIVING IS GIVING.

Cue Rocky theme music please!

Happy helpers

Happy people are thoughtful people. They consider the needs of others. Making a difference takes centre stage in their lives; it's an important part of their identity. Their thoughtfulness is measured in how they treat others, including those they don't know, and in countless silent acts of kindness. If you're not convinced that thoughtful people are both happy and sexy, just ask anyone in a loving relationship with a few years under their belt how sexy thoughtfulness is to them and how thoroughly unsexy its opposite is. I would much rather be with an 'average joe' that thinks about my needs first than a Ryan Gosling only concerned with pleasing himself—the most handsome men can become quite unattractive after a few years. I truly believe you outwardly become who you are on the inside as you get older.

If you Google the world's nicest man, you may find the name Patrick Morgan. Patrick is a custodian in Florida; he works at the airport and found an iPad with $13,000 stuffed in the case. He returned it to authorities and the iPad owner quickly picked up his case, giving Patrick a $60 reward. What did Patrick do with his money? He gave some of it to a homeless woman at the airport and the rest to a struggling co-worker.

My first thought on this story is how little of a reward this iPad owner gave him, but Patrick isn't as cynical as I am—his thoughts were for those less fortunate than himself. He literally put his money where his mouth is. Not only has he been labelled the nicest man in the world, but he was recognised by The Broward County Aviation Department in Florida for his good deeds with a plaque; his employer, Sunshine Cleaning Systems, also gave him a $625 reward for his honesty. I'm not sure I could be as generous as Patrick in this situation, but I certainly hope to be. This is wonderful karma in action—getting publicly recognised for something you do in private.

We all have something to offer. In London train stations around Christmas, they ask people to bring coats for homeless people. The response is incredible. One week, I saw hundreds of coats being delivered by people on their way to work. It was one of those examples of humans at their best: people truly want to help.

In New Zealand, a self-taught mechanic by the name of Grant Magrath gathered a group of mechanics and formed Caring 4 Cars. This organisation collects funds and gathers volunteer mechanics to help fix vehicles for individuals that have difficulty paying for repairs. He found a way to use his skills to help those who are going through a rough time.

My parents did not have a lot of money growing up. There was always enough for food on the table, but that was about it. Yet, they were always helping out people, cooking dinners and dropping them off for people who were doing it 'tough,' as they would say.

One day, my dad dropped me off at school and got out of the truck, noticing a one-dollar bill on the ground. He picked it up and told me to give it to my teacher. I looked around—all I could think was, "How would she know who it belongs to?"—but I did as I was told. My teacher was surprised and said thank you. That day has always stuck with me—it was only one dollar! But that could have bought me lunch that day. It could have been used for gas for our car. My dad knew the right thing to do if something isn't yours, even if you could use it yourself—whether it be one dollar or 13,000.

If you find something that is not for you, don't keep it—find the owner or pass it on to someone else who could use it more then you. You'll never regret an act of real generosity.

- *Exercise: If you think back to the nicest thing that someone has done for you, what comes to mind? Take out a pen and paper and give yourself ten minutes to brainstorm a list of the nicest gestures you have been the recipient of. These are some of mine that came in mind:*
- *My manager yelled at me in front of my work colleagues about a mistake I had made (it was a spelling error). Not only did I feel bad about my mistake, I was humiliated in front of my team. One of the senior publicists came over and gave me a big hug, while everyone else pretended not to notice (I wasn't offended by this—they were trying to be polite). My colleague extended a very warm and kind gesture at a public and vulnerable moment to me, and I will never forget that.*

- *A friend from sent me flowers at work after a particularly difficult time.*
- *A friend, who also happened to be a neighbour, left a care package for me on a date that she knew would be difficult (the anniversary of my father passing away). It was completely unexpected. She didn't spend much money—she literally put together some tea and a card—but it made me feel so loved and cared for.*
- *My first proper manager gave me a shot at work experience when I had no experience and nothing but a smile and a lot of enthusiasm. I will forever be grateful to Ingrid for taking me on, as it was the start of my media career.*

- *While working in retail, I helped a customer find some ink cartridges. I was not doing very well at this job and, frankly, was in over my head working at a computer store when I barely knew how to turn one on. This lady called the store that night (I know, because I answered the phone), and asked to speak to my manager just to compliment me on my customer service, which gave me the confidence and grace to continue in that role.*

CHAPTER

17

Nothing replaces a good ol' fashioned hug (even Facebook, Twitter or emoticons)

"Find out who you are and do it on purpose"
—Dolly Parton

We live in such an hyperconnected world now. With smart phones and all the platforms that come with them—Facebook, Twitter, Instagram, Pinterest, Skype, WhatsApp and countless other messenger services—you can virtually connect with anyone in your life and stay in touch. It's an extremely useful tool when you have relatives and friends living far away and a wonderful way to keep in touch that doesn't require a phone line or a postal stamp. However, the vast amount of technology is making us passive in our connections with people. Technology was made to enhance—not replace—relationships.

I love seeing what my Georgia friends and relatives are up to. Facebook is the best way to do that and allows me to feel connected to what's happening thousands of miles away on a daily basis. But this medium does not replace the relationships I have formed with my family. My mama still makes an effort every Christmas Eve to call all of our relatives (she has seven siblings) to say Merry Christmas. She does this regularly—as well as email, Facebook and Skype on occasion. We use technology as much as we can to stay connected, but nothing beats having a one on one conversation with someone.

THE RESPECT APP: Put your phone away and pay attention to those talking to you

There is a popular cartoon with a couple sitting in a diner. The girl has taped a phone to her head, saying "This seems to be the best way to get your attention." I laughed when I saw this, but oh how it rings true nowadays.

For my birthday one year, my husband took me to a very high-end restaurant on the Sydney Harbour. It was difficult getting a booking and we were both excited about trying it out—it was a real treat, and one not to be repeated any time soon. We enjoyed the night; the food was exquisite, but I looked around and noticed at least half of the tables around us were using their phones. Here we were, sitting in this 5-star restaurant with gorgeous views of the Sydney Harbour Bridge, and people were scrolling on their smartphone and not even speaking to each other or enjoying the dining experience. What a waste!

What social media is not for: keeping a diary. Do you complain about your life on Facebook or use Twitter to rant about a certain person or event that has left you frustrated?

Do you really use Facebook to stay in touch with people or just create an image that everything in your life is perfect? Mental health consultants report that the increase in the use of social media can cause a direct increase in anxiety and fear of personal failure. As Mark Twain famously said, *"comparison is the thief of joy."* Social media can be a wonderful thing—depending on your intention. If you find yourself disappointed in your recent Facebook or Instagram post because it isn't receiving as many likes as you'd hoped for, it's time to take a break and try living #nofilter.

When I make time to see someone—whether it be a friend or relative—I put away my phone. Unless I have an urgent work call I know will be coming through, there are no exceptions. It is rude to use that time to check phones or interrupt our conversations when it dings. There have been times when I have been on call for work and have explained that to a friend when we meet for coffee but, for the most part, the people in front of me are my priority. Not a text, tweet, or post. Be respectful of the people who have taken time to see you and speak to you in person—a luxury in this phone-tapping world.

Unless you are POTUS, an on-call surgeon, or are waiting for life-changing news, there is no reason for you to have your phone on the table when you're meeting someone for dinner, cocktails or coffee. Have some respect for the people who make the effort to come and spend time with you. In the words of Darren Hardy, *"what controls your attention, controls your life"*.

CHAPTER
18

My mama always said...
(Rules for keeping peace)

*"You can be the ripest, juiciest peach in the world and there's
still going to be somebody who hates peaches"*
—Dita Von Tees

This chapter is dedicated to alert you to modern day 'rudisms' and 'nice alerts' that can encourage and remind you of the little gestures in everyday life. It's the little things that make life stressful or special, so choose wisely!

Rudisms

- Texting and walking (also a health hazard).
- Not offering your seat on public transport to someone who is older, pregnant, disabled (yes, I have seen this many times).
- Talking on the phone while at the cash register.

- Not holding the door open in buildings and elevators.
- Sending a text when a tragedy or death has occurred to avoid an awkward conversation.
- Interrupting a person with another thought during conversation. You think what you have to say is more important. It's not.
- Passive aggressive comments. Be direct or be quiet and get over it. No one has time to figure out if you're annoyed with them personally or if you're just having an off day. Act like a grown up.
- Not making eye contact or shaking someone's hand when you meet them or are introduced.
- Ignoring the person who cleans your office.
- Gossip. Whether you're starting it or just engaging with it, it never ends happily for anyone involved. There is a southern term we use—*"Bless her heart"*—that means you don't want to engage or add to the conversation. It's a perfect deflector when someone is trying to bring someone down.
- Being invited to a group birthday morning or afternoon tea and not actually saying happy birthday. We call these 'cake runners'—they take what they want and run, thinking no one will notice (trust me: people notice).
- If someone sends you a card or package, say thank you as soon as possible.
- Ignoring the new kid. Not just rude, but potentially stupid— they could end up your boss one day.
- Yelling or hanging up on a person trying to sell you something over the phone. They're just doing their job—say no thank you and end the call.
- Leaving a party/event without telling the host or saying thank you.

Posting things about other people on Facebook. Social media is not your dumping ground for relationship issues (although quite entertaining, it's not a wise way to deal with it publicly). It's like going to a party and talking about a fight you and your boyfriend had while your boyfriend is standing three feet away from you. Everyone is keen to and will gossip afterwards. Keep your private stuff private.

Nice Alerts

- Ask about their parents. If you don't have a conversation starter, ask about parents: how are they? What do they do? This is polite but also personal.
- When a tragedy or death has occurred, make a phone call, write a card, drop off a cake or send flowers. Do something personal.
- Always take a gift to a party, dinner, lunch or birthday (a bottle of wine, for example, or bouquet of flowers). The host should always feel appreciated or thanked.
- Smile. You have no idea how many people will judge you as nice just on that action alone. One of my flatmates ran into another potential flatmate who was coming to interview. She said she didn't smile and didn't seem 'nice'—this was before the interview even started.
- Compliment a co-worker. Find something nice (and genuine) to say.
- Bake something and bring it into the office
- Tell the person making your coffee that they are doing an awesome job.
- If you think a nice thing, say it to the person you are thinking of.
- Write an email to someone you haven't spoken to in a while.
- Call someone and tell them you love them.

- Think of a favourite memory of a sibling growing up and send it to them.
- Send a co-worker a thank you email for doing their job.
- Volunteer for a charity event.
- Send flowers to a friend going through a hard time, or just a text saying, "You rock!"
- Offer to babysit for a neighbour or friend and give them some time to themselves.
- Give money to a charity/church.
- If you see a homeless person on the street, offer to buy them something to eat.
- Buy a stranger a train ticket.
- Buy coffee for someone you aren't friends with. If you've had issues in the past, it's a great way to bury the hatchet.
- Offer to cook dinner when it's not your turn.
- Write an encouraging email to someone.
- On social media, choose three people and write something encouraging/loving on their page (or DM, if you're shy).
- Send some pictures you know a friend would like.
- If you aren't sure about certain photos with another person, don't post online. Instead, send privately as a group or ask permission first.

If a person in store is really awesome, send a letter to management or follow up with a phone call.

CHAPTER
19

Gratitude always invites more to the table

"Let gratitude be the pillow on which you kneel to say a mighty prayer"
—Maya Angelou

For a few years, I volunteered at a homeless shelter, which involved making dinner and preparing beds for twelve people in Sydney. It wasn't laborious, but when you've finished working for the day, sometimes you don't have the time to prepare a homecooked meal. Volunteers would do various things; some were quite the culinary experts – sadly, I was not one of them. When I did make a pasta one night, I had two guests refuse to eat it – one didn't like mushrooms, the other hated tomato. That's 17% of your dinner guests down right there.

So, after another evening of slaving over the stove when people *"weren't that hungry,"* I decided to go another route and made sandwiches instead. I prepared a spread that had many options and we would wrap up leftovers and give people sandwiches to take with them the next morning. I thought it was practical and seemed to provide people with choices, instead of me just cooking what I thought a group of strangers would enjoy.

Just so you know, I would always bring a homemade dessert (usually brownies) to make up for my lack of home cooking—it seems only fair! People enjoyed the sandwiches and were grateful for the most part. Except for one man. He said he thought it was so cheap that the shelter wouldn't give them 'real food.' He was annoyed there wasn't any lemonade that he could drink.

I usually wouldn't say anything—I knew the people in these shelters were having a rough time—but this particular time? I was taking it personally. I asked him how much he thought this food cost.

"I don't know," he said. I told him the amount. *"That is a lot."*

I then told him the volunteers—meaning me—footed the bill. Not the charity house. He was quiet after that. I didn't expect or want an apology; I really just wanted him to stop complaining, which he did. I did feel guilty for not having something more scrumptious on offer, but it was genuinely all we had the time to do, and I have since learned you can never please everyone. After that one night, I really didn't want to go back the next shift. I did of course—I wouldn't let one person put me off helping others who walk through that door—but that one person had (or I allowed him to have) that effect on me. A single guest was rude, ungrateful, and affected the experience of everyone inside the house. If you can't say anything nice about what someone is doing for you, giving to you, or cooking for you, you can at least give them your manners. Most people are just after acknowledgement and a little bit of gratitude goes a long way.

CHAPTER
20

Check your heart
(Motivation is everything)

"Being true to yourself never goes out of style"
—Reese Witherspoon

People in the South 'call it like they see it.' They are straight shooters and don't have time for anyone who isn't. But they also appreciate the importance of good manners and—unless coaxed to do otherwise—will always use politeness, even in the company of people they don't' take to. You may just think I am advocating for 'suppressing' your feelings about people and pretending to like someone when you really can't stand them; in fact, I'm arguing the opposite. I know people I've worked with—out of a motivation for climbing the ladder or just being liked—will say things or do things that are not genuine, just for a positive response.

I don't call that nice. I call it FAKE.

You know the line *"If you can't say something nice, don't say anything at all?"* It doesn't say *"pretend you like their new dress when you don't,"* or say they did a great job in that meeting when they didn't. People do enjoy being complimented—when it's sincere. I have seen many people giving false praise because they're hoping to get something in return. That is desperate and manipulative.

There is a difference between wanting to encourage someone and wanting to get in their good books. When your intent is to make yourself look good, no matter how much sugar its covered in, it tastes sour.

These people can do well in the office, yes. It's hard to ignore when someone is complimenting you continuously. Don't be that person. If you think something nice of someone, say it! People need encouragement. But if you're just trying to butter your boss up before salary review time? I'm sorry to break it to you, but you aren't thinking like a nice person—you're thinking like a selfish one.

Look, we all have personal agendas. Of course I want to get promoted, earn more money and be seen as the best of the best—but I want to EARN these things on my merit. Most importantly, I want to be authentic along the way.

Also, don't be the person that falls in the flattery trap. If you notice a person who constantly compliments you about things – just think *"Am I the only one?"* Is there a pattern with this person? Do they want something from me? Maybe they don't. Maybe they're just a genuinely nice person and you can learn a thing or two from their actions.

The point is, check your motives. If someone or something doesn't ring true, investigate that feeling. You are a smart woman and your gut is a truth teller when it comes to the people you're surrounded by. Be led by your intuition and not your ego.

Be nice, but be for *real*.

CHAPTER
21

You are just a ray of sunshine!
(Choose your friends wisely)

"Find a group of people who challenge and inspire you, spend a lot of time with them, and it will change your life."
—Amy Poehler

People will either encourage you or discourage you. To be a happy and encouraging person, you need to be careful who you allow into your inner circle. You pick up the traits of those around you. Renowned success leader John Rohn says that *"you are the product of the five people you spend time with."* A recent Harvard study took this idea even further, showing that your salary is the average of that of the five people you spend the most time with. Money talks, honey! Wanna be a millionaire? Stop hanging out with people who are broke or not interested in investing in their future and start going to networking events. Get uncomfortable; mix with people who are ahead of you in their career path and see what happens! Your bank balance will thank you for it.

Who are the five people you spend the most time with? This could be your husband, your co-workers, family members, or your best friends.

I can assure you their thoughts, attitudes and goals reflect your own. If you want to know what your future holds, look at your inner circle; it will tell you a lot about where you're going. I once worked beside a fellow publicist who was a great deal more experienced then I was. I liked her, but she complained every single day. About… anything. Everything. At first, I thought she was going through a rough season (we all do from time to time!), but after a few weeks, I realised this was the filter that she lived her life through: everything was hard and she was a victim. It really hit home when she took a vacation. She was so excited about it and, for weeks, that was all I heard about. She couldn't wait to not be at work; she needed a break and would be staying with a friend. The first day she came back, all she could talk about was what she didn't enjoy: the flight over, her friend had a baby so she could only do so much sightseeing—the list went on and on. All I could think about was how lucky she was to have free accommodation. I found myself coming into work, quickly saying good morning, and then putting my headphones on to avoid conversation. Others may not mind such conversations, but I found it draining and a tad discouraging.

We had another colleague who had the nickname Dementor because it was nearly impossible to be happy around her. She made a talent of complaining and could find the downside of anything; it was draining to be around her.

Misery loves company and you have to be careful as to what company you regularly keep. I would rather be alone and encouraging myself than spend time with people who gossip, complain and bring others down and have no positive outlook on life. Be intentional about who you give your time and energy to.

So, I ask you: who is your tribe? The older I get, the less likely I am just to hang out with anyone for the fun of it. I need to know who I am investing my time in. What is their attitude about life? Do they have goals—are they likely to help me achieve mine? This is not a selfish question; it's a wise one. If you accept every invitation you're given, you may wind up with a lot of Facebook friends, but you'll also wind up with little time for yourself or the people who really matter.

Energy attracts like energy. If you find your friends constantly complaining about their life—for example, if they've complained about their boss for five years but haven't even looked for other jobs—I would start questioning their goals and their impact on mine. Maybe I'm picky. But I know who my tribe is—it's a sacred circle where we exchange celebrations and battles, and I know I can be encouraged or motivated if required.

We all have bad times. I'm not saying not to share these times with people you care about, but they have to earn that spot. You shouldn't just give it freely to the girl you met a church last week. The right people around you can literally change your life. If this doesn't resonate with you, ask yourself this one question: *'After you spend time with this person, how do you feel? Happy? Encouraged? Or drained? Tired and a tad deflated?'* It's a good litmus test for the people in your life.

Exercise: Make a list of the five people you spend the most time with and next to that person write the feeling you get most after having a conversation with them or meeting up socially. How do you feel about life? Are you motivated to pursue your goals? Do you check in with each other, hold each other accountable? Are these people doers or always full of excuses? Do they challenge you (in a good way) to step up in a certain area in your life? These are the questions to ask yourself when you are looking at where you want to be in life and where you are now.

CHAPTER 22

Grace under fire

*'You must find the courage to leave the table
if respect is no longer being served'*
—Tene Edwards

I'm a big fan of speaking your truth. In case you haven't noticed, I like to talk.

This part is going to be painful for some of you to read, but here it is: sometimes we celebrate sharing our feelings, our pain, out hurt—no matter what, because that's just 'me being me'—but sometimes, it's just stupid. Sometimes, it's showing all your cards to people who don't deserve to see them or, worse, won't honour them when you do.

Below are some of my most embarrassing and teachable moments where I lacked the grace I am talking about and, finally, where I learn to show up with it.

Grace and ego

This is the part you've been waiting for: the Hugh Grant story.

I'll save you some time. I was not offered the job. The interview was the most awkward professional experience I have yet to encounter.

Let's just say the meeting was not at all like I had dreamed about.

He wasn't as taken with my American / Aussie accent as I had hoped he would be. He didn't invite me to his country manor to play croquet and dish behind-the-scenes of Bridget Jones's diary.

It was, in fact, quite an unremarkable event... until: my ego was triggered.

I was giving a presentation in a very small cramped meeting room and doing my thing. Mr.Grant seemed less then interested. He yawned, stretched his arms, looked at his watch and, frankly, looked bored as heck.

At first, I tried to ignore it. Then, I couldn't keep my concentration. I felt my confidence shrivelling every second until I reached my breaking point. I finally just blurted it out:

"Mr Grant, do you have a problem with what I'm saying? Because you don't seem to be with me here."

He froze. The room froze. My innermost being froze.

I had just called out a British person on their behaviour which appeared to me to be a tad rude. And you don't really do that— especially when that person is Hugh Grant.

I saw it, but the damage had been done.

He responded in his cool British way—*"yes, I'm with you, I promise"* —and sat up, which was enough for me to continue and get out of the room as quickly as I could.

I allowed my hot-headedness and insecurity to rob me of showing up as the graceful and professional gal I like to be. All because I was a tad intimidated by being interviewed by a famous person with a fancy accent. I likely wouldn't have gotten the job anyway—but I certainly fast-tracked the process because I let my ego and my temper lead in that moment. I was stupid for my unconventional outburst in that moment. It possibly (and unintentionally) shamed him, and made me look unprofessional.

My point is this: pick your moments people. Don't let your emotions get in the way of a good opportunity. It's not a great look on you. And you won't get the job.

PS: My feelings on Hugh

I have a lot of respect for Mr Grant and the work he does to lobby for laws to protect citizens from intrusive media. The only reason he was in that panel interview is because he cared greatly for the work the lobby group did (check out: hackedoff.org if you want to know more). He is also very generous in time and donations to charities he never even gets media attention for. He doesn't need to, or have to, but he puts himself out there because he wants to see a change in the world. RESPECT. I was invited to his birthday party a few weeks later; he was quite the charmer. While I am still awaiting my invitation to his country manor for a cup of tea, my book of Grace says he's a man with conviction: I'll always admire how he uses his personality and influence to try and make the world a better place. Maybe we should all take a leaf out of Mr Grant's book.

Grace and unprofessionalism

When I was working in TV, I had a high-profile programme I was working on with a presenter I was friendly with. She was smart, well-liked, and gaining a lot of traction in her own field as a TV personality.

This time we worked together was possibly one of the most stressful for her, both career-wise and personally. She was nursing a six-week-old baby while launching two programmes; this involved early mornings and late-night interviews, last-minute media requests, as well as her own regular TV commentator gig.

I wanted to help out as much as I could—taking care of her kids and newborn during interviews, saying yes to everything she asked of me –to make her life as easy as possible. That wasn't my job. I was her publicist, not her assistant or nanny—she had one of those, but I was still on-hand in between. But I like to be nice, I saw a need and didn't think a thing about it (boundaries are important, people!).

Until I received an email from her.

Actually, I was cced. She emailed our head honcho, the Head of Television, to rave about the production, the assistants, the editors, the doorman—basically everyone except me—saying how amazing they all were. I didn't receive a single mention.

From a publicity standpoint, we had achieved national coverage. I had also gone way beyond, personally helping her during this stressful time. Whether or not it was intentional, being left out of this email felt like a slap in the face.

I felt ignored, disrespected, and really PI**ED off.

Being the emotional peach I am, I reacted. I was angry, hurt, and took it very personal. I went straight to my manager, who basically phoned in the executive producer on my behalf to say how upset I was.

In that very moment, I knew it—I should have kept it to myself.

Why? Because it made me look like an unprofessional cry baby. Even though I was RIGHT, I was not helping myself.

And, even though I was right, it wouldn't mean that I would get the response I so craved and felt that I deserved from this person (if you haven't noticed by now, us nice gals tend to be a tad co-dependent, which shows up in work relationships too).

What should I have done? Said nothing. Took a walk. Made a mental note not to get so involved next time. Maybe mention it to my manager later in passing as an FYI, not like an emotional puppy in need of rescuing. I could have licked my wounds privately, gone for a run, had a drink with my girlfriends and talked about how crappy it was, and moved on. So that, when I met this person again, I could have known how they valued me and kept it professional from then on.

"But Rachel?? Where's the 'truth' in that??" I hear you say.

Your truth is sometimes just for you, and your wisdom. Speaking your truth isn't always emotionally downloading your own feelings to someone because you just have to get it off your chest. You actually lose the power when you speak from your emotions.

And if you *really* need to download it? Take it to God.

Mandy Hale said: *"Don't waste words on people who deserve your silence. Sometimes the most powerful thing you can say is nothing at all."*

Self-control goes a long way. I'm not saying this from a place of snobbery, trust me. I still struggle with this one.

My lesson here is this: the way you leave a situation is just as important as how you enter it.

There will be opportunities for you to be really offended. And hurt. And to lash out. And to have a heart to heart with someone who really did you wrong. But I'm learning, and have learned painfully, not to give that much energy to someone who doesn't deserve it.

It won't make a difference in some cases.

And the more you can keep your emotions in check at work, the more respected you will be. I'm not telling you to be a robot, but if you need to have a serious chat with someone? Do it from a place of the mature, Queen of awesome and level-headed person you are.

Some of the strategies I have learned that help me are:

- Take a walk.
- Count to ten.

- Take notes before a meeting to keep you on script.
- Pray before I pick up the phone.
- Have a bracelet engraved with 'Keep calm,' or something that reminds you to keep your cool, and wear it every day. When you feel tempted to lose it, switch the bracelet to your other hand.
- Tape quotes to your desk that will help you respond—not react.
- Draft your email response and WALK AWAY. Make yourself a cup of tea and come back to it, or send to a colleague who can edit with you. I have sat on many draft emails because I had to mentally cool down before I could do a rewrite.

Grace and walking away

I once had a work situation where I had to seriously check my ego. I was being treated unprofessionally, ignored and there were things happening that I knew, if I continued to stay in that environment, would affect my reputation and my own confidence.

It wasn't working.

I really wanted to have an authentic conversation with the manager, who was someone I greatly admired, but every time I started this route, something would come up. I couldn't even get five minutes alone with this person, which left me pretty frustrated.

When I made the decision to leave, I felt relief. But then came the other decision: HOW would I leave? Like a huffy teenager and slam the door? Make passive aggressive comments to colleagues on my last day?

I decided I would do everything possible I could to leave on a good note.

This was no easy task, but it was worth it because I felt good about myself when I walked out the door.

I showed grace in this situation by crafting a gracious and professional email to show there were no hard feelings and that I was grateful for the opportunity. I advised of my last day and created a kick-butt hand over and reports that would help continue my work. I smiled, brought in flowers, wrote a personal thank you card, and said how grateful I was for the experience I had there.

It sounds simplistic, but I went out of my way to ensure that I was seen as gracious and professional in a very unprofessional environment. If I had decided to 'speak my truth' on deaf ears, these gestures would have been pointless.

HOW you leave the table is sometimes more important than you actually leaving it. People always remember how you leave a situation. If you rock up to the Christmas party looking like Cinderella and have to be carried out later that night holding your bag and only wearing one glass slipper, guess what the story will be the next day?

Your inner awesome is most challenged when you have people and situations around that will trigger your inner critics: the voice inside your head that says *"I'm not good enough or smart enough or pretty enough or interesting enough."* But it also presents an opportunity for you to show up as *Grace under fire*.

Keeping your cool when people are disrespecting you? It shows their shame and showcases your grace. Because that's who you really are.

CHAPTER

23

Rejection and rainbows

"The way I see it, if you want the rainbow,
you gotta put up with the rain."
—Dolly Parton

I love hearing success stories. I love encouraging and motivating people to pursue a life and career on their terms. But I don't want to leave out a crucial part of this journey.

Rejection.

It really hurts.

While I love sharing my 'crushed it' stories, I want to share with you some moments where I experienced rejection and felt like a total failure.

I was once rejected for a role that I honestly believed I was a shoe-in for. The recruitment process was the longest one I've ever been a part of, and I gave the final interview my all. I walked out feeling like Beyoncé. But when I got the final call, it was a gracious 'no.'

I was rejected. And this one hurt.

I moped around a few days, thinking: *"Why God? What's the point? Why should I keep putting myself out there when it's a no?"*

I felt very sorry for myself, as evidenced by my chocolate binge.

While I was driving in my car one afternoon, I was letting my thoughts run wild about what I had done wrong and why I had even gone for that role in the first place and how ridiculous I was for even thinking that I had a shot (classic victim thoughts, which tend to show up when I am moping).

Then I saw it. A rainbow. One of the most beautiful rainbows I had ever seen.

The next day, I saw another rainbow. Then another. In a period of two weeks, I saw more rainbows then I had seen in my entire life. It was as though God was reminding me—here's my promise. It's still here. Remember my promise to you.

Hope, faith, good luck, whatever you want to call it—that was my symbol, amidst a painful rejection, that God's got all of this. Even when you feel rejected.

Here's the truth: rejection is inevitable. Not just in your career, in relationships, in friendships, in families… it's something we all have to face at some point.

Rejection can sometimes make us question ourselves and the value we bring to those around us. If you don't put it into perspective, rejection can become a roadblock to your destiny when, really, it's part of the path.

When you are going to the next level, expect rejection

You can absolutely protect yourself from this horrid feeling by not doing anything outside of your comfort zone. But on the other side of your comfort zone is awesomeness, freedom and a life that is SO much better for you. All of this comes with a price tag: rejection, with a side of judgement.

When I finished university, I was so eager to get a job and start creating my career. I applied for at least forty jobs, and had about ten interviews before I was finally given my first real full-time PR role in Sydney.

It took six months of serious rejection, casual jobs in retail, lots of late night applications, many phone interviews and interview outfits, reaching out to people, to recruiters, and putting myself out there to get to that one YES.

I knew it was just a numbers game—a test of my own grit.

If I kept applying (to roles I was interested in, that is), I was bound to get a yes eventually. And, when I finally did, it felt amazing. Because it wasn't just any job. It was THE job that God had for me. He had it waiting for me all along. Rejection is part of getting you to your purpose—not detracting you from it.

The good news: you do get used to being rejected by people. It's like a muscle you have to exercise at first, but once you do? You feel unstoppable. So, no matter how hard it feels, keep going—get used to it. And remember: that job wasn't for you anyway.

Rejection is a wonderful life filter that gets rid of the wrong opportunities (and wrong people) from your life.

Rejection is God's protection

This isn't the advice people love hearing (particularly after a bad break up), but I can tell you from personal experience—THIS IS TRUE. I remember being devastated after not landing what I thought was my dream job straight out of university.

It was a total rejection from the job I felt I would have been perfect for that allowed me to go for a job that was way more prestigious, better paid, and just all around a much better role than the one I had been pining for. The point is, if there is rejection attached to something, it's not meant for you. It's that simple.

Jeremiah 29.11 said, *"I know the plans I have for you, plans to prosper and not harm you, plans to give you a hope and a future."* I have had to cling to this truth many times over the years, but my experience and faith shows me every time that God is faithful. When you are using your skills, talents and gifts that He has given you, He will not allow them to go to waste—trust me.

You and God cannot fail. So trust Him. Trust His Word. You are highly favoured. He has a plan for YOU, that will exceed all of your expectations if you just trust him and take action.

It doesn't take the pain out of being rejected – it can be flat out disappointing, but don't allow it to stop you from going again. Have a cry (or a Ben and Jerry's tub, or two) if you must, but then move on—God has something better in store for you.

Rejection is getting you there

Rejection is never easy, but you need to know that it's not a roadblock, but a road sign. A sign to go into a different direction, or to stop, stand still and assess what you need to do next (which is usually keep going).

Maybe there is something practical you need to learn. Maybe you need some support on how to conduct interviews, your resume needs refining, or you need to follow-up with clients more—whatever it is, ask some trusted friends, mentors or colleagues for advice. Don't deal with this alone.

It can be common to think rejection means you aren't meant for that job or career, but it's just part of the process when you're building something or going for something that is outside your normal.

Just ask: *What am I meant to learn here? Where am I meant to go next?* Sometimes the answer will feel very vague. God doesn't provide the road map, but He will give you the next turn off.

There will be an answer. Trust your God-given intuition. Don't overthink it—and don't let it keep you from moving forward.

Have a little grace for you

"A woman knows by instinct or intuition what is best for herself"
—Marilyn Monroe

You teach people how to treat you. This is as true in the workplace as it is in home. If you don't have boundaries and don't take control of your own life, habits and schedule, it is likely you will never have the time or energy to even recognise how you can make positive changes in your life (or someone else's).

I love to run (once I get out of the door, that is!). It's the only exercise I can actually stick to and don't completely dread. It clears my head. I try to do it regularly but, like everyone, I get into a rut sometimes and can go a few days or weeks without my butt getting out the door. I love me some R&R. But I notice a pattern. Once I stop running, I stop eating well. Once I stop eating well, I don't get great sleep. When that starts, I start having only enough energy to make it to work and home: eat, sleep, maybe watch some TV and repeat.

By doing less, I am more tired, less motivated, and more self-focused (I tend to start complaining how tired I am when I am doing very little). When I stick running back into my life, it just motivates every other part.

Once I take care of my physical self, I have the energy and stamina to look outside myself and see where I can be of use, whether that be at work, in my community, family or friends.

I understand we all have priorities—families, busy schedules we try to accommodate every day—but giving your physical self the right attention is one of the most important ways to be nice to yourself.

I grew up in a very church-centred household—everything revolved around church. This was no bad thing. I believe growing up in church gave me the attitude of serving, which would help me with my career in public relations (I often start a professional conversation with *"How can I help?"*). Church teaches you about living in a community, serving others and being there for each other.

That being said, servanthood must be balanced with self-care. You cannot fill from an empty cup.

On flights, during the safety demonstration, the first piece of advice is to always put your mask on first and then help those around you. You will do no one any favours if you help someone put their mask on, then collapse on the floor. The more you take care of yourself, the more people you can help.

Former president Barack Obama starts every morning exercising. Surely if the leader of the free world has an hour to take care of his physical self, we can squeeze some me time into our schedule? If you're constantly exhausted, but find yourself saying, *"that's just the way it is"*—let me burst this bubble for you. No. That's just the way you allow it to be.

Being a nice person does not mean being pulled in ten different directions until you're run ragged and you haven't had time to book an appointment at the hairdressers in six months. Being nice does not mean being a martyr. Nor does self-care mean self-pleasure. There is a balance, but you have to strike it. This advice may sound general, but that's because it's as personal and individual as the person reading this book.

How do you know when your balance is out of skew?

Well… for me, it's when my temper gets a little shorter. It's when I don't find joy in the morning, when all I can think about is how much I have to do. It's when I haven't had time to speak to my husband for more than ten minutes in a day.

Self-care for one person might be reading a book; for someone else, it could be seeing a movie or catching up with a friend or catching a game of golf. These things should not be seen as luxuries. I know I am a nicer person to be around when I am running regularly and exercising. These things somehow keep everything in perspective and I just feel better about myself.

You must be nice to yourself and prioritise yourself, because no one else will do that for you.

For a while, I used to have an attitude with people who practised strong self-care and would think, *"Well, that's good for them. They have time to do that."* It took me a while to figure out that the only difference between me and the lady across the street who looked like she had it all together was better time (and, therefore, life) management. That lady was nice to herself by knowing what to say no (and not feeling guilty for it), fully showing up for what she said yes to and ensuring she could enjoy herself along the way.

You have just as many hours in the day as Beyoncé, so let's start showing up for ourselves every day, not expecting anyone else to give us the break we should be giving ourselves.

Five things more important than your career

1. **Your loved ones.** Let's face it—when all is said and done, these are the people who will be there for you when times get tough. My dad died when I was twelve, which was devastating, but gave me a newfound respect and love for my family. Make time for your parents or send a text to your siblings and make a plan for dinner.

   My sisters and I lived all over the place for years, and we held regular Skype wine nights. Now that we live much closer, we have regular catchups. I know I'm lucky, but I genuinely love spending time with my family. When my husband and I both worked full-time, he regularly travelled for work; we agreed to a proper date night every two weeks, no matter what was going on in our schedules. Now that we're parents, that's a harder date to keep, but we try. Your friendship circle also gets smaller the older you get and it's harder to cultivate friendships, so make time for your besties. Your village of loved ones, like your career, require work to keep them strong.

2. **Your health.** Gosh, I wish this had clicked earlier. When I get stressed, I turn to food. When I started working in television, everyone drank—after a good day or a bad one. The combination of always working and usually combining my social life with work took a toll on my health. I was sick more often, sluggish at the best of times, and lived off caffeine and sugar. I gained a lot of weight and just stopped enjoying life because I wasn't taking care of my most precious asset: my body.

   It wasn't until I made a decision in January 2015 to run a half marathon (and signed up for it after a few wines one evening) that I had to cut out time for my body and cut down on the things that were abusing it: sugar, caffeine, wine.

This would also prove to be one of the most important and challenging six months of my career—I was working at the BBC during an election campaign. The hours were longer, the work incredibly intense, but running kept me sane and the vices I were drawn to were not as needed as before. I lost some weight and crossed the finish line of my first (and probably last!) half marathon four months later. I needed that monumental task so I would finally stop putting off excuses that 'work is too busy' and make my body my priority.

My favourite tip: set yourself a sleep curfew. Yes, just like when you were a child. I realised that I need to be in bed by 10pm every night to be my best self the next day. I now add a humidifier full of eucalyptus oil and listen to a meditation app before I go to sleep to create a more nurturing experience for myself.

3. **Your passions.** I love writing, but when I would come home very late in the evenings my mind was drained and I didn't have anything else to talk about except work. It wasn't until I started setting a curfew for my work phone—that is, turning the phone off at a certain time (not just before I went to sleep)—that I could properly 'switch off' and start reading books again and start drafting my own.

Travel is also another passion. I always had a list of places I wanted to go (and still do), but there were times when it was too hard work wise, let alone money wise! All I would think about is the amount of work I would have to come back to. When I finally decided to go backpacking in Europe in my early twenties, I was fully expecting to have to resign from my job, but I knew

I just needed to do it. I was fortunate—they allowed me to take my eight-week trip and come back to work—but they would never have offered such a break unprompted. I just had to take it.

Trust me, you will never regret any investment you make into something you are truly passionate about—even if it means an absence from your day job for a while.

4. **Faith.** I grew up in a Christian household where church was the norm. In my early twenties, I skipped church for a while but have always kept my faith and would regularly study the bible and pray.

I am at my most centred when I am part of a community of like-minded people that share a similar belief system. When work was taking over my life, this is one of the first things that would get crossed off my list; however, I now know it is essential for my peace of mind.

Whatever your spirituality is—whether it's a religion or meditation that connects you to a higher being—practice it first thing every day. You have to feed your personal life first before feeding your career.

5. **Volunteering/Serving.** It can be difficult finding somewhere to volunteer when you are working full-time, but the rewards always outweigh expense. When working in Sydney, I volunteered once a month at homeless shelter. I would be lying if I said I was always excited to go, but meeting people who were really doing it tough—from drug users to people who were just struggling to make ends meet—was a serious reality check for me. It gave me gratitude for the life, career, and shelter I had. Science has also proven you literally get a 'happy high' when you do something

for someone who cannot give you anything back. Giving back is essential to getting a life.

Exercise: Make a list of the things you LOVE to do, that make you feel happy and complete. When is the last time you did them? Put one of activities on your calendar so you are doing something joyful every day. Make it a habit, not a luxury. You gotta have something to look forward to everyday!

Generosity invites opportunity

*"My mother told me to be a lady. And for her,
that meant be your own person, be independent"*
—Ruth Baider Ginsburg

K arma isn't always instant, even though it always seems to be in the movies. The bad guy always gets his 'comeuppance,' just in time for the hero or heroine to get their fortune and live happily ever after.

I would be lying if I said pay-off is instant. It rarely is, but it does come—often in ways you cannot imagine. I have lived through examples of this and can personally vouch for how manners and a nice attitude can completely transform your life.

Be nice and land a job

My very first job out of university was doing public relations at a small town hospital. I loved it, but I was looking for full time work and had been going to a few interviews (okay... many).

I was in the running to get a role at the Australian Medical Association, which would have been an amazing first job. I was highly doubtful I would get it, but I did. It was a good salary, a lovely team and I loved the job. I knew my manager wasn't completely sold on me when I was interviewed.

Months later, I was at a board meeting and recognised one of the board members—she used to work at the hospital I had been temping at. She was little, dressed in crazy colours; I honestly thought she'd been a patient or volunteer.

Not only was she on the board of the AMA (the role I now had), she had been called by my now manager about this particular job. I barely remember speaking two words to this woman, but she had told my manager to *"just give me the job"* as I seemed nice enough and smiled a lot. I never had a conversation with this woman, and she recommended me for a job that would change the course of my career.

Be nice to a stranger and gain a friend

Years ago, when I was living in Sydney, I was catching the train to go to City2Surf (not run, just walk!). Being an American in Australia, you always notice fellow Americans, but after years of living in the city, I had learned to keep to myself.

This time felt different for some reason. I struck up a conversation with a fellow American who was travelling with her family and we kept running into each other throughout the day. I made a very good friend that day by the name of Andra—just by asking, *"Where are you from?"* A wonderful friendship would soon blossom from those four words. Being polite can bring in the people who are meant to be in your life—just look up from your phone once in a while.

Be nice and gain a reputation

One of my first jobs out of high school was working at a photo lab at a local retail store. It was hard finding part time positions and I was grateful for the work—it was close to home and I enjoyed developing pictures.

One of my colleagues also happened to be a schoolmate, so I thought it would be a good working environment. Boy was I wrong. From day one, the girls on the team were abrupt, rude, and not all helpful. I was good at the job and helpful with customers, so I could not figure out why I felt so despised by these girls.

I stuck it out (mostly because I needed a paycheck) and kept a smile on my face as much as possible. I later found out six months down the track that my supposed schoolmate had said some unsavoury things about me before I started working there. It felt like I was back in high school. I didn't know her all that well, so it was a real shock.

One day, a team member said to me, *"You know, (insert name) said some things about you before you first started, but you are not at all how she described. It really has made me question her and why she would do that."*

My jaw nearly dropped to the floor. I hadn't realised the very person I thought would be my advocate was in fact my enemy but, more than that, me just getting on with my job and being polite revealed something about her character. I said little, smiled a lot and did my job. And, after a while, that wore people down. People finally saw me for who I was.

As Michelle Obama says, *'When they go lower, we go higher'*. Kill em with kindness—it's a timeless remedy that can work in almost every situation.

Be nice and have fans forever

In the south, we don't seek to humiliate people. Even when they're ignorant. We'll smile, keep quiet, but never bring attention to someone's inadequacies. It's just not how we were raised.

A few years ago, comedian Martin Short was interviewed on a morning show by Kathy Lee Gifford. He was talking about a recent film he was in and, near the end of the interview, Kathy asked about his wife. She went on about how they had such an amazing marriage together and how much she loved his wife. Martin kept smiling and said a few words that she was good. Unfortunately, Kathy Lee or her producer had overlooked some vital pre-interview research: Martin's wife, Nancy, had died of cancer a few years prior.

Kathy later released an apology, but Martin never said a word about it—he was so polite and didn't want to embarrass his host, even though that question must have been hurtful for him to say the least.

There is always something to be said for not publicly humiliating people with how wrong they are. You will always be remembered for your response, and his response was cool, humble, and very, very nice.

Be nice and be healthy

For four weeks, researchers from the University of British Columbia assigned people with high levels of anxiety to do kind acts for other people at least six times a week. This included things like holding the door open for someone, doing chores for other people, donating to charity, or buying lunch for a friend. The researchers found that doing nice things led to a significant increase in people's positive moods. It also led to an increase in relationship satisfaction and a decrease in social avoidance in socially anxious individuals.

A recent scientific study reported that an anonymous 28-year-old walked into a clinic and donated a kidney. It set off a pay it forward ripple effect, where the spouses or family members of kidney recipients donated one of theirs to someone else in need. The "domino effect," as it was called in the _New England Journal of Medicine report_, spanned the length and breadth of the United States of America; ten people received a new kidney as a consequence of that single anonymous donor.

Be nice and land a client

When I first started coaching, I signed up to a certification program that required me to get a certain number of hours before graduating. I was over the moon excited to get started, so I decided to offer some of my friends free sessions just to get started.

One of my friends asked if her colleague could also use a session. She was going through a break-up and feeling stuck in her career. I was nervous, but said yes. The session with her colleague went so well that she ended up being a paid client—just like that. By offering a free service of value, I landed a client. By the end of working together, she landed a new job with more pay, a loving relationship, and a much happier and authentic lifestyle.

And that wasn't the last time that happened. I tell my clients now, particularly when they're starting out: Serve first. Offer value.

Whether on a Facebook live, or in a meeting room, or on a blog. It's the best type of attraction marketing you'll ever be involved with.

CHAPTER

26

You can take the girl out of Georgia, but you can't take GA out of the girl

"As for those grapefruit and buttermilk diets,
I'll take roast chicken and dumplings."
—Hattie McDaniel

I haven't lived in the South for fifteen years. I have since lived in Sydney and London; I'm pretty much a city girl now (and I love it). But once a southerner, always a southerner. Here are some things that, no matter where I go, remind me of where I came from.

- Baked goods, such as brownies, are acceptable presents in any situation.
- You know the kid's names of everyone at work, from the security guard to your boss's secretary.

- Hugs are like handshakes. You get used to handshakes, but still go into hug people when you meet them and hope they reciprocate.
- You keep a stack of thank you cards at work and at home; you never know when the occasion will arise for a handwritten note.
- You smile. At everyone. This has led to many interesting, and sometimes uncomfortable, conversations with strangers on streets and on trains. You say *"I'm just smiling"* a lot.
- The Starbucks staff think they're your best friends. You are always happy to see them (because it means this is an awesome way to start off your day.
- Iced tea sold in cans seems sacreligious.
- You can recite Dr Phil quotes when discussing relationship issues with your friends and seem oh so wise.
- You are at your most polite when you can't stand a person: you use your best manners and think of your grocery list.
- You put on makeup when you go to the grocery store.
- You would never, ever be seen brushing your hair in public or putting on your make up outside the bathroom—that's just unladylike.
- You love Lynyrd Skynyrd; their songs always remind you of a family reunion somehow.
- You are perfectly happy sitting around all day doing nothing and don't understand why people keep themselves so busy.
- A shared recipe is more precious than gold (and it comes with a story!).
- Even when it's a sauna outside, you always take a cardigan to church.
- When you host a meeting at work, you bring candy/sweets for everyone. It just seems strange inviting a group of people

together and not having something to offer them (even in a business meeting). This both delights and confuses attendees.

As well as writing emails, you still write thank you cards to bosses and colleagues when a situation arises.

CHAPTER

27

Don't let your mouth overload your tail (Lovers of talking, listen up)

"Confidence is silent, insecurities are loud."
—Anonymous

I remember getting my report card and proudly taking it home to my parents. I used to love to read the comments—I was usually a good student and complimented by my teachers. Then I hit the fourth grade. Something changed. I read in horror the comments my teacher had written about me: *"Rachel has been distracting other students by talking. She won't stop talking in class, even when asked to be quiet,"* or something of that nature.

I could not believe it—I was just telling stories and chatting to other kids! Little did I know I was starting to develop in my future career. I studied a degree in Communications and worked in journalism and public relations, so my 'art of talking' would greatly benefit me in years to come! I like people and seem to find conversing with anyone quite natural. It's an asset for my job. Yet, my mouth has also gotten me into more trouble than I care to admit.

When I was in school, I was on the bus and a particular guy who was a few years older than me was looking at me oddly. He was being annoying in my sensitive teenage opinion and I thought he was trying to get my attention, so I asked what his problem was. When he didn't answer, I said the first thing that came to my mind: *"What are you, deaf?"*

Bingo! Yes, he was deaf. And about 95% of the bus heard this lovely comment. I felt horrible. I couldn't believe how insensitive and stupid I was. I tried to apologise later, but it wasn't all that effective in this instance. It was sincere, but still it didn't help with my 'nice' persona—the damage had been done. It was a throw away comment that came from me always speaking my mind. That was a 'please swallow me into the ground' episode. Others are not as harrowing but certainly memorable.

My family had planned for an important birthday present for my mom—she was turning a big number and we wanted to fly her close friend in from Georgia for a visit. We were all going to contribute and it would be a grand surprise, giving her time with a person she loved dearly. One day, Mom was on the phone with her friend and I overheard the conversation. Mom started saying *"you're coming over here!"* and *"I can't wait—we're going to have the best time together!"* She was gesturing wildly and getting very excited. I was getting anxious. When Mom got off the phone, she said her friend was coming and she was so excited. I couldn't believe it – the birthday surprise was ruined! I told my sister and we told our stepdad that we had to tell Mom what our plans were.

Maybe you can guess what happened next. We told Mom. Her friend had not said a word on the phone. The whole thing had been Mom's idea—no plans were made.

I ruined the surprise by talking and assuming. My family wasn't too happy with me. I wasn't trusted with a secret for years. You may be able to have more constraint over your mouth meeting your brain that I do; I literally have to bite my tongue on a daily basis.

I have yet to get in trouble for things I did not say. I may regret not speaking up at some point or leaving information out, but this never did a disservice to my reputation—or more importantly, to those around me.

The real art of communication comes when knowing to be quiet. As Simon and Garfunkel said: silence is golden.

CHAPTER
28

The Keanu effect

"The simple act of paying attention can take you a long way."
—Keanu Reeves

Keanu Reeves was a popular actor throughout the 80s and 90s. Personally, I loved *Point Break* and *Speed*, but everyone has their own favourite film of his. He seemed to 'tetter off' after having some personal tragedies, but has been making a comeback in recent years with films like John Wick and even a brand new Matrix movie set to start filming—arguably because of his reputation as a nice guy.

A clip went viral on social media of Keanu on the NY subway. He is sitting on the subway like a normal person and notices a girl standing. He offers his seat; she accepts. He stands up. No more words are exchanged. The clip went for about 30 seconds and went global. The comments were incredible; all of a sudden, people viewed Keanu as the 'nicest man in Hollywood'.

I do agree that this was a nice thing to do, but why should we expect anything less, whether you are a Hollywood start or average Jo on the street?

The lesson here is this: you have no idea what 'effect' your polite everyday gesture will have, not just on those around you but your own reputation.

Just think of the 'Keanu effect' – you cannot buy this amount of positive publicity, but it will stick with you for years to come.

How would you act if you knew someone was filming you secretly in everyday situations? Be like Keanu.

CHAPTER 29

The Truth About Grit

I don't know exactly what's next but I'm stepping forward with grit, anchored with grace
—Julie Graham

When I was 12-years-old, my dad died.

It was sudden, unexpected and left my mother a widow at 40 years old with 3 teen daughters to raise.

You never get over losing a parent so early in life.

It creates a scar that feels so visible – even 20 years later, I can feel the excruciating pain of the moment I was told my life would never be the same again.

I remember seeing his face for the last time, when he dropped me off at school that day.

If only.

For years I lived in the 'if only'.

He had one semester left of finishing a college degree (while working full-time as a prison guard).

He had a side business which was doing well enough that he could quit working for the prison and go into full-time business.

If only.

But here's the thing about the 'if only'.

It's like the Erisad mirror in Harry Potter - the mirror which shows not the person but their deepest heart's desires. Harry see's his dead parents and spends hours each night staring at the mirror. The wise Dumbledore later says to Harry:

" This mirror will give us neither knowledge or truth. Men have wasted away before it, entranced by what they have seen, or been driven mad, not knowing if what it shows is real or even possible."

Some people are so stuck in what could have been, they are missing out on what opportunities are right in front of you.

The 'If only' in your life will rob you of what God has next for you.

I can tell you this from experience.

There will always be MORE in the next chapter available for you.

More opportunities, more love, more happiness, more connections, more memories, more joy, more ideas, more ventures, more offers.

Just more.

It may not always feel that way.

I'm sharing something vulnerable here – in a book about kindness and success and hustling your heart out it may seem out of place – but you need to hear this truth.

There is something that you have gone through (or maybe you are going through right now) that has devastated you. Broken you. Made you question every single thing on this planet and for a while maybe even stolen your hustle. And your joy. And made you a little hard.

I want you to know I have been there.

And I'm not going to ignore that pain you have.

But I'm going to offer you a choice here: one that I had to make a long time ago.

Don't let it break you. Let that pain drive you.

To more. To showing up. To trying something different. To dare to believe that something AMAZING can come out of the horrid things you have experienced.

It's a decision to live that way. I lived the other way for so long – stuck in misery and the land of 'if only'. And it was heavy and life sucking.

I finally decided to try something else. Like pretending to be happy. And caring. And letting the loss of my Father drive me to building His legacy, not pining in the loss for years to come. My Father became my biggest driver. His commitment to building something for our family. To hustling. It's real. It makes me keep going. It gives me strength when I have none. It gives me grit when I feel imposter syndrome hanging over my head.

I am choosing to let that part of my story drive me, not define me.

So, today I say to you-

Honour the pain in your life and what it has allowed you to become.

But let it be your comeback story not your 'if only' moment.

We all love comeback stories.

So, be a comeback story. It's much more authentic then pretending like life hasn't touched you in the hardest way.

And people really like to be around that kind of grit – in work and in life.

It's the most inspiring and compelling stuff of the human spirit.

CHAPTER 30

What Would Dolly Do?

*"If you don't like the road you are walking,
start paving another one"*
—Dolly Parton

I'll announce my bias here: I grew up in the Deep South. Dolly wasn't just a singer or actress, or a cultural icon. She was someone we could relate to: you could see yourself talking to her at a hair salon, or asking to borrow a cup of sugar (yes, people still do this). She wasn't just an institution—she was our Dolly.

The tagline *What would Dolly Do* has become a popular print in the south. It's not that surprising, given she was as part of the southern culture as grits were on eggs (apologies for the southern culinary reference). Dolly is an icon—an actress, singer, songwriter—who has been in the industry for more than fifty years. She has continually reinvented herself, collecting new fans and keeping her old ones, not by changing her look or going for a new song style (as opposed to other people in the music industry, who seem convinced it is the only way to remain relevant). She remained true to herself, and happy to parade her southern ways.

She is everything a southern woman wants to be: comfortable in her own style, honest, self-deprecating and happy to give the time to anyone she meets. In this day and age, it's good to have someone who can epitomise the values of kindness and charm, even with their legendary status. It hasn't gone to her head. She knows where she came from. She's not pretending she is someone she isn't, and she knows the best publicity she can give herself is being her charming polite self. I can't think of another global celebrity who has been in the industry longer than Dolly Parton who hasn't had scandal follow her. She has the same amount of scrutiny that anyone in the talent arena does, but she handles it like a pro and continually stays on top.

Sometimes, when I find myself in a tense situation or a difficult discussion with someone, I think, *"How would someone better at this handle this? Who do I want to be?"* Sadly, I was not given the same talents as Ms Parton, but we had an upbringing steeped in similar values: be honest, be direct, be polite and charm if at all possible.

Whoever it is that you see as the 'epitome' of your values, as the role model for your version of success, think: *"What would this person do? How can I get out of this situation what I need with my reputation intact and end on a friendly manner?"* That should be the question you ask before every meeting, difficult conversation, work review, family confrontation and so on.

Dolly works for me because I can relate to who she is trying to be. Your role model could be Princess Diana, Michelle Obama, Sheryl Sandberg—any strong person that has the life and attitude you would to see more of in yourself. Whoever it is that appeals to you only does so because you have those skills and talents yourself. You just have to acknowledge that part of yourself and recognise that the more you intentionally behave that way, the more natural it will become for you.

Let's be honest: we are all on a journey to be the best version of ourselves we can. I'm not going to start dressing in platform heels in sequins (it's not in my job description, thankfully) but it is helpful to have a role model who has success and a good reputation. Closer to home, my number one role model is my mother; she taught me the values of humility and compassion towards everyone. She's not one to hold a grudge. Many times when I've had issues in my career and had no idea what to do, I would just call my mom and she would give some of her Mama advice, as relevant today as it was many years ago. Be honest, reliable, and kind always—even when you need to be firm. It's difficult to practice, but also difficult to argue with this logic. She's a genuinely happy person, which is a rarity to see these days, and people enjoy being around her. Even when she's having a bad day, most people wouldn't have a clue because it doesn't change how she treats people—it's just who she is.

When I was visiting our hometown in Georgia, I was in the local JCPenneys and a lady who used to work with my mom came up and hugged me (just cause I was Barbara's daughter!).

"*I want to show you something,*" she said, and went out the back to her desk. She came back with a yellow post-it that looked quite tattered. "*When my Mama died—ten years ago, now—your mother left this on my desk. I have kept it there ever since and when I'm having a bad day, I look at this post it and it makes me smile.*"

The message was a short, encouraging note, reminding her of the love that was around her. My mother wouldn't even recall writing that note—it was something she did quickly before leaving work for the day—but that gesture continues to have ripple effects to this day. You never know how one gesture will impact someone.

Myself? Well, I have a ways to go. I am no Ms Parton, but I'm committed to living out these nice principles every day. Sometimes I fail horrendously, but I try and have enough self-awareness to apologise and do better tomorrow.

Nobody's perfect, nor should we expect anyone else to be.

Sometimes, you need an old-fashioned reminder of what is important in life. Opportunities are around you all the time to make an impact on those around you, but you have to make space in your thinking about it. Every day, we should actively look for opportunities to be a blessing. Remember to be kind. Nothing can beat or replace this quality or way of life. The more we have of it, the better we are, the better the world is and the better quality of life we have—and the more doors will open to you professionally and personally.

Am I really that nice of a person? I try to be, but I don't think I am anything special.

And I wrote this book as much of a reminder to myself as it is to those reading it. It's easy to sometimes think, *"No one cares about being nice—why should I?"*

The answer is simple: you make a difference. And people do notice.

These strategies, manners, gestures—whatever you want to call them—have helped me stand out in the workplace. I am nothing special, but the acts themselves can be invaluable to those receiving them. It leaves a memory. The more kindness you bring in your life, career, and relationships, the happier and more successful you will be—I guarantee it.

When it's time, don't hesitate

Knowing I was finished with my PR career was one of the hardest truth bombs I had to face.

I landed what I thought would be my dream job working for the BBC—I thought I had finally 'made it.' But after my first day, I realised that this was not what I wanted to do anymore.

I had worked for years, pining to get to this moment in my career. And here I was, walking home after my first miserable eleven-hour day.

On the way, I picked up a burrito, bottle of wine and chocolate bar to help dull my misery. I shovelled food into my mouth and stared blankly at the TV, thinking *"What's wrong with me?"* It was a baffling, scary time.

I kept going. I thought that if I could just climb the ladder, things would get better. I landed my first manager job at thirty and assumed that finally getting that brass ring would make me happy.

Sadly, that wasn't the case. My purpose for years had been to build a career I was proud of, earn a good income, travel the world, save money and work for incredible companies that had impact. I had achieved these things, but I was ready for more—and had yet to figure out what 'more' meant for me.

I wasn't just bored; I was unfulfilled and aimless. I needed a change.

I began writing for publications and started my own coaching and copywriting business while working at my full-time job. I stepped out of the boat of 'career success' into the unchartered waters of entrepreneurship. That story in itself could warrant a book, but I mention it here because you need to know that, when it's time to move on, you should never hesitate. Whether it's a job, career or relationship, women have strong intuitions. It's our best and most unique quality—we know instantly when something doesn't feel right.

When it's time to move on… don't make excuses to stay. When a relationship has run its course, don't cause more pain by ignoring the inevitable conclusion. And—when you find yourself constantly overwhelmed, having regular migraines and suffering Sunday dread every week (like I did, because I avoided the truth of my situation for 2 years)—don't ignore your body. It's telling you everything you need to know.

Entrepreneurship was not in my original vision, yet the principles were the same. I wanted to love my work, make good money, have more flexibility in my schedule and have a global impact. The *how* is what changed. My version of success changed.

And it was the best decision I have ever made. I get to work on my time, on my terms, on my rates. I get to serve incredible women who are total game changers and be involved in their transformations—all over the world. I get to have the impact I always wanted. I get to be paid to be me.

Being authentic is about recognising when the thing you are in is no longer working for you. When you're feeling high and dry for too long for a career or a relationship or business, it starts to leak out.

No matter where you are at now, make sure you love it, or love what it brings to you. If it's money, great—if you're happy to work for just a paycheck, good for you. But if you know you're meant for more, and just don't know what that looks like, be kind to yourself. Be honest.

If it ain't working for you anymore, stop fighting it. Ask yourself: *"What is the next step here?"* Imagine how you want to live, wake up, spend your days. What is the legacy you want to live?

Life is short. You are awesome. If you aren't feeling awesome, it's your job to find out why and to take the steps to get there. I made it my part-time job to find out what was next for me—praying, seeking, and researching myself became my biggest priority, one that paid off with the clarity of my next step.

If you're thinking of leaving your current job or situation, check out my website www.lifeonherterms.com, where I share a ton of resources that will help you out.

Giving up my PR career was the hardest, but most authentic thing I have ever done. It was freeing. True, authentic success exists when you love what you do and how you do it. As the famous Johnny Carson said, *"when you love what you do, you never have to work a day in your life."*

Work at loving your life. After all, we only get one shot to do it right. With some grit, God's grace, and a lot of hustle, I am proud of the career and business I built and continue to build for myself.

I wasn't perfect—no one is—but I like to think I did it the best way I knew how and genuinely tried to treat others right. And, like you, I'm a work in progress. There's always a next level. Just be sure to lift others as you are climbing that ladder. After all, that's the way my mama raised me.

When you're looking at going to the next level in your life and career, change is inevitable. It's also confronting, uncomfortable and messy. But it's also what leads us to our next breakthrough. Don't resist the change. Comfort is where our dreams go to die.

Make a promise to yourself and write it at the end of this book: promise to never stop reaching, to lead with grace, to never stop asking yourself what you are meant for and to keep going in that direction. Promise to make joy a priority every day, to work on your relationships—even when it's hard—to go for that job, to ask for that raise, to start that business. Promise not to settle for second-best in any part of your life. You are too amazing, too incredible, too inspiring, and full of so much peachy awesomeness to settle for anything less than you were created for.

Hustle, sister. Show up for yourself and make no apology for knocking on every door you can see. God will use every action you take, every conversation you have, every phone call you make, every email you send, every prayer you pray, to take you exactly where you are meant to be. And it's so much better than any career plan you've thought of so far. His dreams for you will surpass any you have for yourself.

Just say yes. And take action, expecting amazing things to come your way. God has got something so exceptional for you because you are exceptional. There is nothing you can dream that God can't make happen. When you put your faith in Him, when you take heart-led action, when you live with grace for others, when you take a leap outside your comfort zone—you're telling yourself and the Creator you're ready for MORE.

The opportunities are endless; your talent, experience and heart is what the world so needs right now.

CHAPTER
31

Thank you kindly
(A note to the reader)

Dear Reader,

Thank you so very much for taking time out of your busy schedule to read my book! I know you are a kind person because, frankly, you made it to the end, which is a real honour for me. I'm so humbled that you were interested, even a little bit, in what I had to say. I believe kindness starts at home and whatever you give in the world will come back to you—one way or another. It has been a real pleasure talking about some of my workplace memories—the good, the bad and the ugly—and I hope it has inspired you in some way, or even encouraged you. Even if you may not have the fanciest education or come from the right side of town, if you have manners, treat everyone with the same respect and give a little bit more value than what is required, your world will get bigger—opportunities will come your way. I'm not being a positivity princess here, just someone who has experienced doors opening in places I never thought possible because I never forgot where I came from and never got too big for my britches. Old-fashioned manners are more important than ever and are a must if you wanna succeed like a classy gal in this modern era. My final piece of advice: if you are ever in doubt of the next step, the answer will always be a single question. *What is the kindest thing to do here?* Start with that, bake some brownies—the rest will follow. Also, watching *Fried Green Tomatoes* always helps.

Wishing you love, success and peaches

Rachel x

Want more stuff like this? Join my Facebook group, Life On Her Terms https://www.facebook.com/lifeonherterms to get more resources and connect with other awesome gals like yourself who are totally going for it.

My Bio

Rachel Reva is a PR consultant, copywriter, coach, author and founder of Life On Her Terms. She worked in the media industry for ten years as a news publicist and PR manager. Her career has spanned television, health policy and election campaigns, both in Australia and the United Kingdom. She is also a contributor for several global outlets, including *Huffington Post* and *Goalcast*. When she isn't writing, coaching or stalking Oprah, she is planning her next holiday. You can follow her on Instagram @lifeonherterms.

CPSIA information can be obtained
at www.ICGtesting.com
Printed in the USA
BVHW041048040421
604164BV00023B/2858